Writers, Writing on Conflicts and Wars in Africa

Edited by

Okey Ndibe and Chenjerai Hove

Published by

Adonis & Abbey Publishers Ltd
P.O. Box 43418
London
SE11 4XZ
http://www.adonis-abbey.com
Email: editor@adonis-abbey.com

and

The Nordic Africa Institute, Uppsala
P.O. Box 1703
SE 751 47
Uppsala, Sweden
http://www.nai.uu.se

First edition, 2009

Copyright 2009 © Okey Ndibe, Chenjerai Hove

British Library Cataloguing-in-Publication Data

A catalogue record for this book is available from the British Library

ISBN: 9781906704520 (HB)/9781906704537 (PB)

The moral right of the author has been asserted

All rights reserved. No part of this book may be reproduced, stored in a retrieval system or transmitted at any time or by any means without the prior permission of the publisher

Writers, Writing on Conflicts and Wars in Africa

Edited by

Okey Ndibe and Chenjerai Hove

Contents

Foreword .... *vii*

Chapter 1
Introduction
Okey Ndibe and Chenjerai Hove 9

PART ONE
WRITING, TELLING AND DRAWING

Chapter 2
Contemporary Projections: Africa in the Literature of Atrocity (*Aftrocity*)
Yvonne A. Owuor.. 17

Chapter 3
Writing Between the Spaces of Conflict
Okey Ndibe 27

Chapter 4
Small People, Big Wars: A Personal Memoir
Chenjerai Hove 33

Chapter 5
War and the Written Word
Juliane Okot Bitek... 43

Chapter 6
The Nigerian Writer and the Niger Delta Crisis
Ogaga Ifowodo 49

Chapter 7
A Lizard Grows Another Tail: The Persistence of War in My Writing
Thabisani Ndlovu 57

Chapter 8
Seasons of Tragedy and Hope
Michael Woodman 69

Chapter 9
Africa's World War: A Congolese Journey
Kevin Eze 81

Chapter 10
Cattle raiding in South Sudan and the shadow of war
Skye Wheeler 91

Chapter 11
Preachers on the train
Munyaradzi Makoni 101

Chapter 12
The journey home: suitcase or coffin?
Lauryn Arnott 107

Photographic documentation of Lauryn Arnott's drawing titled
Journey Home, **February - December 2004** 113

PART TWO
REFLECTIONS AND CONVERSATIONS

Chapter 13
"Literature on Demand?" Violence and the Literary Imagination in Contemporary Southern African Fiction in English
David Bell 123

Chapter 14
"I can speak if I want to speak ... Would you hear me if I called?" The Politics of Representation and the Poetics of Reception in *What is the What: The Autobiography of Valentino Achak Deng*
John Masterson 137

Chapter 15
Fictional Works of Ayi Kwei Armah as a Basis for Democracy and Reconstruction in West Africa
Anna Chitando 157

Chapter 16
Engaging the Deaf through Song and Poetry: The Dilemma of the Nigerian Artist in a Season of Political Anomie
Hope Eghagha 165

Chapter 17
Reflections on *Inyenzi*
Andrew Brown and Karin Samuel in Conversation 171

Notes on Contributors 184

Index 189

FOREWORD

This collection put together and edited by two accomplished writers and teachers, Okey Ndibe and Chenjerai Hove, is a kaleidoscopic "wordscape" containing creative perspectives on issues of violent conflict and war in Africa. It is not only about the muffled cries of the victims—often too many, and too weak to defend themselves or speak their pains to those in power, but also about the trials of writers, artists and yes, witnesses, who have to tell stories of the woes of war; however not just war, but also the hopes that may yet spring from its ashes.

The stories, images, reflections and essays that you will find in this book flow from the proceedings of the presentations and deliberations of the Creative Writers' Workshop on War and Peace in Africa, organized by the Nordic Africa Institute's programme on Post-Conflict Transition, the State and Civil Society in Africa and the Dag Hammarskjöld Foundation, and held in Uppsala, Sweden, from December 1 to 2, 2006; and a further call for contributions from across the world along the same broad theme. It also opens up new vistas to the entire discourse of peace-building, healing and the reconstruction of war-shattered societies in Africa. Some of the contributions speak to intimate experiences seen through the eyes of various generations, and even children of war—that are now much older, seeking to make sense of the violence that is often visited on hapless victims, and how wars and atrocities are constructed by the human mind and hands—the very same 'tools' that are needed to transform war to peace.

By bending literature and the arts in general in the quest of understanding and explaining violent conflict and wars in Africa, this collection adds a creative dimension to extant discourses of peace-building, which are largely dominated by discourses drawn for the social sciences and international relations. By bringing a creative humanist perspective to bear on war, it is hoped that the full extent of the human tragedy that war bodes, will be brought home to underscore that words, images and stories may indeed be mightier than the panga, bullets and bombs. And that beyond the various ceasefires, peace conferences and fragile peace agreements that underpin discussions in Africa's war theatres, the often-voiceless victims will survive, and have their say and day, to dream that peace will return to their once-restless minds and lands, even if the scars remain.

Cyril I. Obi
Leader, Research Cluster on Conflict, Displacement and Transformation
The Nordic Africa Institute, Uppsala, Sweden.

Chapter 1

INTRODUCTION

Okey Ndibe and Chenjerai Hove

This book's initial impetus sprung from a convocation of African and Africanist writers and scholars organized during the first week of December, 2006, by the Nordic Africa Institute in collaboration with the Dag Hammarskjold Foundation in Uppsala, Sweden. Tagged "Creative Writers' Workshop on War and Peace in Africa," the conference sought to provide a space for creative writers to foreground their participation in the discourse of war and peace.

Even before the conference ended, the organizers and participants recognized that the anthology of perspectives and experiences that were being generated deserved wider dispersal and dissemination. While conflict is often central in literature, it is somewhat rare that writers who have been touched by war – or by the unease that predates or spawns it – are asked to gather together to meditate on that experience and how it informs their art or scholarship.

The Uppsala workshop over, we were charged with editing its harvest for publication as a book. In that process, we were able to glean patterns, continuities as well as discontinuities in the variety of papers and stories. In the end, we decided to arrange the papers into two broad pods, the one encapsulating personal reflections and anecdotes, the other containing more scholarly offerings.

In carrying out our task, we soon realized that, whilst the Uppsala writers' forum yielded extraordinary insights, a book that was based only on the conference would not achieve the thematic aspirations and catholicity of appeal we felt the subject deserved, and demanded. This judgment led to a decision to call for contributions from a wider field, but retaining the focus on the modes of representation of conflict. The call proved a sagacious decision; we received submissions from, among others, a medical doctor detailing his work in Darfur, Sudan, one of the world's festering conflict sites, a Ugandan writer whose images of the horrors of war are tinged with stubborn nostalgic vistas of a beatific childhood, an artist from Zimbabwe who tells the pain of separation from the homeland through vivid drawings and paintings, and a scholar who gives a gripping insider's account of studying philosophy in a Jesuit college as confusion, chaos and gunshots reign in the Democratic Republic of Congo (DRC). There are also some conversations with writers telling stories of war, struggle and love. This book then is an entwined album, layering the papers and stories we shared over three days in Uppsala with the narratives of writers who deploy a variety of idioms to vivify their experience of the relationship between creative work, conflict and war in Africa.

If wars begin in the hearts and minds of men as they use language and other forms of human communication (and miscommunication) to create conflict, where else to begin in the diagnosis and healing than with the poets, story-tellers, singers, artists, painters, dramatists and essayists who know how to paint, in words, images and movement, the colours and smells of the scars left behind after every conflict.

That was, essentially, the exploratory journey of the Uppsala convocation, the seed that germinated into this book. It was, in many ways, a celebration of the power of words, but in others, an expression of the artist's capacity to doubt so many things about the fragility of art in the midst of conflict where bullets don't flower anymore.

For those of us who were privileged to join the conversation, and undoubtedly for those who listened in, the workshop more than lived up to its ambition to "give voice to the stories, songs, images and messages of creative writers, artists and critics, and bring African literature through the serene scenic beauty of Uppsala in winter to the Nordic world."

Cyril Obi, who served as the conference's central moving spirit, had envisioned it as a "forum [that] would contribute towards the dialogue between critical constituencies, open up new vistas and opportunities for understanding the creative spirit and celebration of life that underpins the dreams, tears and joys, the resilience, survival and triumphs of African peoples in the face of daunting everyday and global challenges." He wanted the participating African writers to underscore their "unique contributions...to the struggles for social justice, peace and development."

Part of the workshop's uniqueness and cache lay in its breaking of new conceptual grounds. African writers are frequently at the centre of the continent's crises and wars, often as bearers of scars – being primary and deliberately targeted victims – but also as bearers of witness. Sadly, they are all-too-often shut off from forums where the meaning and consequences of conflicts are discussed.

True, some African writers make the tragic choice of suborning their witness, even lending their talents to the powers-that-be out to dehumanize and debase their fellows. However, the vast majority of the continent's writers—and here we include poets, novelists, dramatists, memoirists and journalists—have served, and serve—in the words of the conference organizers—"as the voices of the voiceless, holding up the mirror to reflect the true face of self and society..."

Ironically, African writers are hardly invited to make interjections or register their interventions at the plethora of conferences that are organized each year around the theme of their continent's bazaar of woes, conflicts and wars. It is as if the organizers of these conferences wish to consign the writers to minding their purely "literary" business. This stance is both misconceived and informed by a grave misreading of the historical data. The idea of pure art, an art uninfected or uninflected by the surrounds of political upheavals and pervasive social misery, is a myth. Art is shaped by, and shapes, all facets of experience. Each writer's aesthetic outlook is shot through by her or his ethics.

African writers, like writers elsewhere, respond to the stimuli, provocations and challenges of their specific political and economic realities. Their art seeks to reflect as well as transform their people's immediate and historical experience. They vivify, as the organizers of the workshop in Uppsala recognized, Africa's "beauty, scars, oppression, inequities and hard-earned victories." By the very nature of their vocation, writers commune with the people. Their stories, poems, and recollections touch others, and leave them open to be touched in return.

Art is often engaged with the task of reinforcing memories. African creative writers discharge this burden "in song, prose, poetry, drama, pictures and paintings," wrote the Uppsala organizers. In doing so, they risk "arrest, detention and torture, at the very worst, death, or life in exile." Even when the artist is not subjected to exile, detention, torture or death, art remains a powerful and potent tool. It is a transformative instrument, a veritable vehicle for engaging (again to quote the conference organizers) "the struggle for survival, identity, equity, dignity and freedom. It is also about the celebration of life in peace and without fear."

Several of the participants at the Uppsala Workshop embodied the varied drama of the writers' direct involvement in conflict. Dennis Brutus, the South African poet whose back bears the scar of an apartheid bullet, lent a measure of revolutionary gravitas and hard-earned moral capital to the workshop. When Brutus spoke or read his poems, his voice, though slightly enfeebled by age, still rang out with stunning range and power. Chenjerai Hove, his spirits intrepid despite the travails of loneliness, was the workshop's raconteur-in-chief. He told his stories, and that of other fighters against repression, with zest and verve, aware that memory is the exile's ultimate weapon and comfort.

Other absent "spirits" haunted the workshop. As we shared our stories and insights, we had the sense that other African writers, intellectuals and revolutionaries, some of them dead, needed acknowledgment. Such martyrs as Amilcar Cabral, Agostinho Neto, Steve Biko and Christopher Okigbo have a claim on our attention whenever we discuss the writer's role in Africa. These writers and intellectuals had laboured in the African vineyard, and they had made the supreme sacrifice. We also had for company and encouragement the examples of resilience and fibrous struggle provided by the likes of Nelson Mandela, Wole Soyinka, Lewis Nkosi, E'skia Mphahlele, Ayi Kwei Armah, Ngugi wa Thion'go, Jack Mapanje, and Emmanuel Dongala – writers who have paid dearly for championing noble causes.

What emerged from the Uppsala Workshop was recognition of the importance of inviting writers and literary scholars, African as well as non-African, to weigh in on the predicament of conflict and wars in Africa. Each speaker at the workshop touched on the complex confluence of forces, domestic as well as global, that produces and sustains conflicts in Africa.

Writers mine conflicts at all levels for some of their most psychologically rich, dramatically arresting, and emotionally complex creations. By their very nature, conflicts and wars can lend tension and gravity to a writer's outlook. But a writer is not so fascinated by conflict that she or he fantasizes about consecrating it as the norm. A writer ultimately looks beyond the anxiety and unease of the moment and towards some vision of humane enlargement, to borrow a phrase from Wole Soyinka. The writer's search is not for the stabilization of conflict but for some form of resolution, a healing of the breach.

A writer cannot be too sentimentally invested in conflict—for conflicts also constitute a hazard for the writer. Conflicts prey, often decisively, on a writer's imaginative work. This may well provide a psychological explanation for why writers are drawn to the exploration of the character, meaning and impact of conflicts. Conflicts frequently ravage the writer's spirits, sometimes to the point of compelling the writer's delicate sensibility into shocked silence. Just as frequently, conflicts displace the writer, cast her or him into physical or spiritual exile, or even dislocate that sense of centeredness that is essential to the creative enterprise.

The African writer faces no more deadening challenge than the savage unsettlement that is a by-product of war and repression. Many a speaker at the workshop underscored this insight. True, the African writer is far from unique in this respect; all around the world, writers are besieged to one degree or another. Even so, the huge feast of wars and political conflicts in Africa translates into a plague for the continent's poets, novelists, dramatists, journalists—and indeed the broad spectrum of conscientious intellectuals.

The Uppsala Workshop provided participants with an opportunity to bring their unique light to the vexed question of the paradoxical relationship between art and conflict. Some gave highly personal and anecdotal account of their engagement with the hydra-headed monster of conflict. Others offered analytical interventions based on examination of African writers' texts dealing with the subject of conflicts and strategies for resolution.

"If only the politicians who declare wars could read poetry, novels, listen to the songs of the sorrows and pain of war," one participant was heard to say.

Those of us who were in Uppsala, and those who were not there but have now contributed to this book from different addresses, are beginning a conversation that is of the utmost significance and pertinence in a world filled with possibilities for recreation. Taken together, the contributions collected in this book amount to a rich harvest of perspectives and witnesses, and an invaluable, if not unique, contribution to the literature on African conflicts and their resolution.

PART ONE

WRITING, TELLING AND DRAWING

Chapter 2

CONTEMPORARY PROJECTIONS: AFRICA IN THE LITERATURE OF ATROCITY (*AFTROCITY*)

Yvonne A. Owuor

This chapter is titled after a rant piece that may have become very self-indulgent, frankly. I confess it was prepared in a state of rage at the *Economist's* usual hectoring from a holy ground attitude in describing the so-called African condition. You know how trendy it is to describe our continent as poverty stricken, Aids infested and hopeless? And if we are not doing helpless victim things we are slaughtering each other.

However, I shall share with the reader a little bit of the "Africa as the breeding ground of bestial war atrocities" media imaginings that are old. Moreover, given that this is a creative writing forum, ideas swirling out of the underlying questions situated within the topic also beckon. I shall endeavor to reflect on one or two contemporary war and violence concerns.

And finally, space permitting, attach for the reader a brief excerpt from one of my short stories called *Weight of Whispers*. It is the story of a man unable to gaze at the violent disintegration of his life until he stares into his mother's grave.

Without looking at headings, and even if the names referred to are eliminated, you and I can always tell a particular global media piece which narrates the experience of war or violence in Africa, can't we? The details given to particularly abhorrent deeds (not to minimize the excesses or to excuse the horrible deeds—but it is particularly descriptive where Africa is concerned):

You all know the catch phrases: Tribal, ethnic, savage, slaughter, barbaric, excesses, hacked to death, tore the flesh off, horrific, marauding, corrupt, bribed, for some reason--chiefs, armed men, machete wielding, genocide in Rwanda, hatred, brutal, warlords, blood dripped off the walls. *The horror, the horror*, wrote Joseph Conrad. And since then it was more comfortable to determine that darkness of heart was purely African, rather than resident in the souls of the diabolic adventurers.

For example *http://www.irinnews.org/*

"In addition, Rwandans, some of whom took part in the 1994 genocide in the country, have turned against their Congolese "hosts"; committing atrocities that would shake the most hardened heart. Observers say that all armed groups have committed acts of sexual violence and rape but that the Interahamwe from Rwanda have been largely responsible. Since 2002, a German technical aid body GTZ (Deutsche Gesellschaft für Technische Zusammenarbeit) has been documenting the various forms of sexual violence on residents in South Kivu. The violence includes rape by individuals and gangs; incidents in which entire families are forced to watch their wives and daughters being raped, as well as forced incest. In addition, GTZ has documented victims who have had cassava stalks or gun barrels repeatedly rammed into their vaginas. Some were also shot in their organs.

The Economist (Nov 29, 2006) is, of course, reliably consistent in its manner of reporting anything African:

MACHINE GUN bullets zipped over the concrete walls of the Supreme Court building in Kinshasa on November 21st, as an angry crowd of flip-flop-shod street boys and plainclothes soldiers bellowed for justice. In the chaos, the policemen and UN peacekeepers, who should have been guarding the court, ran away. The demonstrators then set part of the court on fire and ransacked the courtroom. The next day, Joseph Kabila, who last week had been declared the winner of the presidential election, furiously gave his main rival, a former rebel named Jean-Pierre Bemba, 48 hours to remove his 600-strong private army from the capital. ...

Warlords in the provinces

In the north-eastern region of Ituri, a vast gold deposit covered by gentle green hills, murderous militiamen have become murderous soldiery. There they prey on peasant miners and increase the prospect of a return to the ethnic slaughter that claimed around 50,000 lives between 1999 and 2003. A long, rattling drive to the south, in North Kivu province, is a warlord general, Laurent Nkunda, who shows little interest in ideas of state expansion. Formerly in the *RCD*, and before that in Rwanda's army, he claims to control 20,000 square miles (52,000 sq km) of wooded hills. As the protector of North Kivu's long-persecuted people, General Nkunda has a just cause. But then, so had many of the actors in Congo's complicated war—and still the result was a slaughter. So long as Congo has no state to address pressing local complaints, its future is an open question.

You also recognise the descriptions of war and violence that describe mostly Anglo-Saxon Protestant endeavors: high morale of the troops, peace agreement, Commander-in-Chief, tried to reason with rebels, collateral damage, heroic, precision, target, few casualties, strategic detail, B52, armed convoys, secured the area.

You get the idea: one set of people do outrageous vampire-like things, suck blood and growl, the other are rational, precise and never indulge in heinous aberrations and crimes that offend the fundamentals of creature decency.....like Abu Ghraib.

Right? I thought that the arrival of Bush's axis of evil might change the vocabulary and transfer slime, gore and machetes into a new species called Terrorist.

Don't get me wrong, I am not complaining, defending or lamenting anything. I am simply curious. Why do many interpreters of global information blithely need to define people - mostly of the darker hued variety - in complex, arcane description of otherness? I am curious about the seething inner realities that require that such projections are directed at 'The Other,' particularly the extreme 'other' forcibly symbolized by Africa and Africa-ness.

There is certainly a place for the idea of the other, but arguably, this is mainly in so far as the reflection on and of the *Other* allows the *I* to understand self. The problem is that the line between staying within the realms of self-understanding and racing into high pedestals of judgment—are faint indeed.

(Mea culpa!)

In the exploration of human excesses, in the admittedly few arenas I have ventured into mostly in Europe and the US, I noted that audiences were far more comfortable and voluble about stories from Ituri, Apartheid South Africa, Darfur and the favourite branded horror 'The Genocide in Rwanda'. I, on the other hand, wanted to hear about the interrogations of the whys and therefores, stuff that had been excavated from the soul of the human experiences of war and violence. There have been terrible laboratories to draw from: World War I, The Boer War, the African expeditions mislabeled 'The Scramble for Africa', World War II, or Vietnam, Bosnia or Chechnya and the invisible, terrifying, very modern, largely invisible War on Terror.

Mostly, I have wanted to join expeditions that seek to archive the vaults of collective silences, past and present. The hush from and about the concentration camp that is Guantanamo Bay resounds and convicts. Today it is the obscure subterranean world war that means that alleged 'high-value' prisoners are moved through secret camps across seas into interrogation chambers in numerous countries. Stories are slipped in with vague words like *"extraordinary renditions"* to describe war and violence gone underground. The horror fades away, captive to transitory memories. That is the problem with projections; it fogs the place between truth and hypocrisy.

Moving on

Drawn from the thought areas that are likely to emerge in our encounters, it is essential, I believe, to contemplate the implications of segmenting human realities and awarding grades to ghastly manifestations and awful gestures of the human soul. Is it any wonder that the mystery of evil and its commensurate sorrows remain a perennial heart and the home of unarticulated misery in the world? Is it any wonder that the vocabulary of anguish tends to lurk hidden within hearts where reality resides with loneliness and voicelessness before horrors that we cannot understand? Do we ever wonder at the suicides of the most articulate ones, the deeply sensitive ones who were penetrated by war and violence at its most insidious — prophets like Primo Levi? What it points to are depths of anguish which so transfigures that it cannot be fully breached so that those who cry for peace can actually believe their desiring.

We understand that the violence of war are deeds of passion. Do peace actions respond with an equal and magnetic virulence? Does peace carry the same strange attraction that violence affords the human being?

I say 'we', but I may be making a terrible assumption that we all give a damn about the state of life of the collective human soul. That we are as passionate about the grandest dream, the daring-to-die-for-peace as Dag Hammarskjöld was. I say 'we' hopefully, because the gist of this piece is simple, it is this: *Nothing human is alien to me.* And just as I am capable of a grand love, a yearning for peace, I am also able to summon all the hounds of war and scream abuse and hatred and use my finger to trigger a gun's explosion.

I wonder if the fear of looking into the reality of who we are and what we are capable of as human beings makes it necessary to look elsewhere to explain the horror that demands confrontation. You believe, as I do, that the magnitude and implication of this theme can, in no way, be restricted to a specific geographical dimension.

Joseph Conrad's horror is easy to find.

Some rhetorical questions: In this beautiful country, do you have armament plants? A missile manufacturing facility? Bullet-making factory? Bomb development unit? Security experts? Do you have a list of people whose profession is 'Arms trader'? You have a standing army? *What for?* Gardening? Preparation for Inter-galactic invaders? Or is all this a preparation to kill human beings somewhere - massively - humans perceived as a security threat? Why are we still afraid of one another? So afraid that it is easier to plan to kill.

(Fear. Interesting territory that. Fear and the ideology of absolutes have a way of keeping populations mesmerised and manageable, don't they?)

That word, 'security' - it needs a long and special interrogation. How widely and wildly it is used to justify all sorts of violence. We need to secure ourselves? From who? Always other human beings. Name the threat.

When we strip the so-called 'Terrorist' *(that whole territory of naming in order to reduce the reality of humanness)* of his mask and bullet or bombs, strip him or her down to the skin, we have a mere human being who loved, laughed and hoped at a point in his or her life. Who yearned and sought. Who believes? Even in madness. And madly, passionately, he or she (re)acts.

Are we that terrified of one another? Is the question about the embarrassment of our fear of the Other? Or perhaps the fear of the memory of the other? The unresolved guilt, shame, an ancient terror of a blood-stained past that has neither been wept over nor purged. There are few answers, admittedly. But there must exist some unspoken insights into the nature of the magnificent being called human who does such wondrous things that extend the boundaries of beauty and possibility and who also does such odious things that push the boundaries of evil.

I don't know. What I do know is that *Nothing human is alien to my nature.*

This war, this violence is ours. Ours is the hateful thing - a roaming stain that prowls through the society and sows seeds of chaos - that thing that appalls our within-ness. And horrifies us with the blood it wastes. Spilled like spit. We are sickened by its methods and the reasons it infects us with, to cause anguish to another. It is a colourless, raceless thing, yet its culture is singular and recognizable. When leaders entrusted with vision announce 'weapons of mass destruction' where there are none, when CNN gloats over so-called 'victory' over an already devastated country where bullet wounds were being treated with aspirin, when activists turn their gaze away when a now rabid leader uses race as the excuse to make of his people refugees. When a man in a cave activates young men to bomb an American embassy and calls the 200 Kenyan casualties, 'collateral.' When we see pictures of young men in orange suits who are bound, blinded and gagged and say nothing.

> What makes loneliness an anguish is not that I have no one to share my burden, but this:
> I have only my own burden to share.
> (Dag Hammarskjöld)

On another tangent:

The stuff of nightmares exorcised on pages so the human instinct for story can be satisfied, looking to human experience as source material for scribbling. The rhapsody of the human being raptured by searingly jarring notes. There is always something that sits wrong in an otherwise perfect universe. A writer needs an antagonist, you know.

Here is a story:

Once upon a time, a man who held a different opinion about life was accused, scourged, beaten and had thorns pressed into his head. A Roman Procurator before whom he barely stood said to the waiting ordinary folk: Ecce Homo?

Behold the man!

Naturally, seeing the sorry face of humanity before them, the ordinary folk wanted nothing to do with him. So the procurator acceded to requests that he be crucified. But the action of the Roman procurator is interesting. He called for water and washed his hands. There is an historical rumour that he spent the rest of his life calling for water and washing his hands until they bled.

The stain. The hunger to purge when we are conscious of a disorder in which we are, somehow, implicated.

Ecce homo.

What then is this human beheld?

> Tomorrow we shall meet,
> Death and I -.
> And he shall thrust his sword
> Into one who is wide awake.
> *(Dag Hammarskjöld)*

An answer is sought. In all our ramblings there is something fundamental we seek.

The answer to the question of the meaning of life, that we seek to gaze upon *Wide Awake*.

And who better to ask than a man who has decided that 10 million people who call God by a different name are vermin to be eradicated? What makes a human like that? In the canvas of writing, though it is right to wail for the decimated 10 million, we can also stare at the man who decided to murder them. Who are you? You whose humanity I share whether I like it or not? You, who by your choice, has implicated me.

The prerogative of such creative writing is that one can take this man, even if he has killed himself, put him on the page and interview him. I imagine an exploration of war and violence in the place where it is all brewed and executed. Within each of us in the thin line delineating choice.

The Gestapo, as you all well know, would not have been successful in the attempted annihilation of a vilified people were it not for the J good neighbours, honest Dutch, French people who submitted names, numbers and revealed hiding places. The Interahamwe succeeded because ordinary moderates, like you and I, went berserk — for a season. Yet when you encounter the killers in the Rwanda Gacaca courts, most are as bewildered and weighed down with sorrow, more than guilt, just as so lyrically presented in the profile on South Africa's Edward de Kock (*A Human Being Died that Night*). But neither they, nor the rest of us who listen searchingly, can find the essential word to give an adequate name to what happened.

I started with a mild rant about the use of words to separate and judge shared human enigmas. I also imagine that for those involved in the creative articulation of experiences, there is also a great opportunity to existing in which to have an intense dialogue with the numerous archetypes of violence or evil that inhabit each of our cultures and shadier imaginations: Shadows, Demons, Ogre, Tokoloshe's. We call them by many names, Satan, Dr. Frank-N-Furter, the serpent in the Garden of Eden, Hannibal Lecter, Hel—the Norse queen of hell, perhaps Loki, vampires…

A chance to excavate silences for the grail of the perfect word that might trigger the relief we seek from selves we have known, seen, felt and feared violently.

Excerpt from 'Weight of Whispers'

The collection of teeth on the man's face is a splendid brown. I have never seen such teeth before. Refusing all instruction, my eyes focus on dental contours and craters. Denuded of any superficial pretence; no braces, no fillings, no toothbrush, it is a place where small scavengers thrive.

"Evidence!" The man giggles.

A flash of green and my US$50 disappears into his pocket. His fingers prod: shirt, coat, trousers. He finds the worked snake skin wallet. No money in it, just a picture of Agnethe-mama, Lune and Chi-Chi, elegant and unsmiling, diamonds in their ears, on their necks and wrists. The man tilts the picture this way and that, returns the picture into the wallet. The wallet disappears into another of his pockets. The man's teeth gleam.

"Souvenir." Afterwards, a hiccupping "Greeeheeereeehee" not unlike a *National Geographic* hyena, complete with a chorus from the pack.

"Please...it's...my mother...all I have".

His eyes become thin slits, head tilts and the veins on his right eye pulse. His nostrils flare, an indignant goat.

A thin sweat-trail runs down my spine, the backs of my knees tingle. I look around at the faceless others in the dank room. His hand grabs my goatee and twists. My eyes smart. I lift up my hand to wipe them. The man sees the gold insignia ring, glinting on my index finger. The ring of the royal household. One of only three. The second belonged to my father. Agnethe-mama told me that when father appeared to her in a dream to tell her he was dead, he was still wearing it. The third ...no one has ever spoken about.

The Policeman's grin broadens. He pounces. Long fingers. A girl would cut her hair for fingers like his. He spits on my finger, and draws out the ring with his teeth; the ring I have worn for 18 years - from the day I was recognised by the priests as a man and a prince. It was supposed to have been passed on to the son I do not have. The policeman twists my hand this way and that, his tongue caught between his teeth; a study of concentrated avarice.

"Evidence!"

Gargoyles are petrified life-mockers, sentries at entry points, sentinels of sorrow, spitting at fate. I will try to protest.

"It is sacred ring...Please...please." To my shame, my voice breaks.

"Evidence!"

Cheek: nerve, gall, impertinence, brashness.

Cheek: the part of my face he chose to brand.

*

Later on, much later on, I will wonder what makes it possible for one man to hit another for no reason other than the fact that he can. But now, I lower my head. The sum total of what resides in a very tall man who used to be a prince in a land eviscerated.

Two presidents died when a missile launched from land forced their plane down. A man of note, a prince had said, on the first day, that the perpetrators must be hunted down. That evil must be purged from lives. That is all the prince had meant. It seems someone heard something else. It emerges later on, when it is too late, that an old servant took his obligation too far, in the name of his prince.

We had heard rumour of a holocaust, of a land hemorrhaging to death. Everywhere, hoarse murmurs, eyes white and wide with an arcane fear. Is it possible that brothers would machete sisters-in-law to stew-meat size chunks in front of nephews and nieces?

It was on the fifth day after the Presidents had disintegrated with their plane, that I saw that the zenith of existence cannot be human.

In the seasons of my European sojourn, Brussels, Paris, Rome, Amsterdam, rarely London, a city I could, then, accommodate a loathing to, I wondered about the unsaid; hesitant signals and interminable reminders of 'What They Did'. Like a mnemonic device, the swastika would grace pages and, or screens, at least once a week, unto perpetuity. I wondered.

I remembered a conversation in Krakow with an academician, a man with primeval eyes. A pepper-coloured, quill-beard obscured the man's mouth, and seemed to speak in its place. I was, suddenly, in the thrall of an irrational fear; that the mobile barbs would shoot off his face and stab me.

I could not escape.

I had agreed to offer perspectives on his seminal work, a work in progress he called 'A Mystagogy of Human Evil'. I had asked, meaning nothing, a prelude to commentary:

"Are you a Jew?"

So silently, the top of his face fell, flowed towards his jaw, his formidable moustache-beard lank, his shoulders shaking, his eyes flooded with tears. But not a sound emerged from his throat. Unable to tolerate the tears of another man, I walked away.

Another gathering, another conversation, with another man. Mellowed by the well being engendered by a goblet of Rémy Martin, I ventured an opinion about the sacrificial predilection of being; the necessity of oblation of men by men to men.

"War is the excuse", I said. I was playing with words, true, but, oddly the exchange petered into mumbles of 'Never Again'.

A year later, at a balcony party, when I asked the American Consul in Luxembourg to suggest a book which probed the slaughter of Germans during World War II, she said:

"By whom?"

Before I could answer, she had spun away, turning her back on me as if I had asked "Cain, where is your brother?"

What had been Cain's response?

To my amusement, I was, of course, never invited to another informal diplomatic gathering. Though I would eventually relinquish my European postings - in order to harness, to my advantage, European predilection for African gems - over après-diner Drambuie, now and again, I pondered over what lay beneath the unstated.

Now, my world has tilted into a realm where other loaded silences lurk. And I can sense why some things must remain buried in silence, even if they resuscitate themselves at night in dreams where blood pours out of phantom mouths. In the empire of silence, the 'turning away' act is a vain exorcism of a familiar daemon, which invades the citadels we never change, we constantly fortify. Dragging us back through old routes of anguish, screeching: "Your nature relishes fratricidal blood."

But to be human is to be intrinsically, totally, resolutely good. Is it not?

The devil laughs at such protestations.

Chapter 3

WRITING BETWEEN THE SPACES OF CONFLICT

Okey Ndibe

A writer enjoys a paradoxical relationship to the notion of conflict. Conflicts are at once essential to the writer's business—his effort to forge imaginative meaning out of chaos and tumult—and, often, a challenge to his humanistic vision. Conflicts impinge on my daily experience as a writer, a member of multiple social communities, as a human being. For me, life itself is stamped by conflicts. Conflicts are ubiquitous, pervasive and, all too often, pernicious.

Conflicts are at the centre of the writer's labours. They are akin to the fiction writer's capital, the preferred stock of his trade. Those who make it their business to fashion fiction often nurture a professional stake in conflicts.

Among the writers who have an extraordinary claim on our attention are those whose works are distinguished by their penetrating power, their insight into social strife, convulsions and disquiets of human conflicts. These writers manage to offer us visions both of our bestial compulsions as well as our capacity for achieving heroic heights.

In fact, in a world where no conflicts erupted between people or within their souls, we would hardly have the great literary dramas bequeathed to us by William Shakespeare, Dante Alighieri, Wole Soyinka, William Faulkner, Mazisi Kunene, Gabriel Garcia Marquez, Chinua Achebe, Nadine Gordimer, Ayi Kwei Armah, Okot p'Bitek, Mariama Ba, and the numerous griots of the world. It is possible to argue that great literature may be woven out of an unsullied world endowed with unremitting goodness. The trouble is that we would then be telling the story of angels, not of humans.

Part of my concern as a writer (and I suspect that this problem confronts every writer to some degree) is how to mediate between literature's fascination with the convulsions of conflict and the writer's intuitive abhorrence of anything that vitiates social vision, degrades the human or discounts salient values.

This predicament is of the utmost poignancy, in part because the writer is an integrated being. I am not a writer only when I am writing and then something else the rest of the time. My tasks may vary according to the vicissitudes of mood, inspiration and opportunity, but every role I play is an expression of a core human ideal. I am not at all sure that this claim is true for other writers. I am far less sure that it speaks to the experience of a medical doctor, or, say, for a lawyer whose first obligation lies in securing the best outcome for a client.

I came into writing precisely because I was wounded—scarred deeply in spirit—by the world that swirled around me. It was, and is, a fallen world, a world on which the deforming hand of savagery has been brought to bear. I have dared to use a word, *fallen*, that is branded with ecclesiastical resonances. And it is indeed a deliberate choice. The world I see both in my everyday encounter with life and in my fiction is one that constantly betrays its promise. It is as if, invited to stand tall, we constantly fall short.

A writer who sees the world in this light, as an arena rife with dangerous detours, paths forsaken, roads not taken, may be accused of possessing and purveying bleakness. He may be seen in some quarters as a trader in jeremiads, a retailer of acidic narratives, a bringer of bad news, a spoilsport.

I plead not guilty. What I do, deploying the idiom of fiction, is to write between the margins of conflict. That way, I draw attention, yes, to the fact of our nasty, brutalized world; but I also, even more crucially, point to the imperatives of humanistic enlargement. It is important to me to show the ruins of the garden. Yet, in doing so, I am already seized by a different dream. It's a dream about the making whole, about restitution, the rebuilding of what has been shattered.

I was born in 1960, a mere five months before Nigeria became independent—a word that today evokes all kinds of ironies. Six years later, Nigeria slipped into a series of catastrophes that led, inevitably, to a full-blown war. That carnage, which entered the lexicon of violence as the Biafran War, is perhaps the single most significant experience of my life.

My sentience was coming into its own as the war erupted. From that war came my first cache of horrific images, a macabre harvest of metaphors underscoring the depths of human depravity. My young eyes beheld images of strafed streets and mangled cars. Day and night, I was aware that enemy jets could swoop at no notice and wreak havoc. I walked about with an unyielding tightness about my belly. My stomach burned daily with pangs of hunger. Driven by necessity, we improvised around food. We relished rats and lizards. We savored plants and insects that nobody, before the war, had ever imagined as edible.

I saw other children who were even worse off than I, their heads big and bony, eyes sunken, bodies emaciated, bellies extended as if with sheer air. Once, standing with my parents at a centre where food and other relief materials were being distributed, I saw a man topple and hit the ground. The voyeur in me wanted to observe it all, but my parents rallied to shield me from seeing. The fallen man, another quiet, anonymous casualty of war, was quickly removed.

In mid-January of 1970, just days after the cessation of the shooting phase of the Biafran War, my parents arrived in Onitsha with five war-scarred children. We were refugees.

Our address had a settled reputation as a historical town. Not only does it nestle on the banks of the River Niger, one of Africa's great bodies of water—and the inspiration for the name Nigeria—it was also famed as one of Africa's largest commercial hubs. But that history was unknown to me at the time—and I hazard it was of little consequence to my parents. We were too enmeshed in a death-suffused drama to care for the town's legend and rich history. Mortified pilgrims, we were weary of spirit and broken-bodied, preoccupied with the grim business of—to use a phrase popularized by Nigerian novelist, Cyprian Ekwensi—surviving the peace.

We were camped out in a sprawling camp in this once idyllic town known as much for its commerce as for the pristine beauty of its streets. Our neighbours were other down-on-their luck survivors of a war that cost two million lives—and took a heavy toll on the nerves and dreams of millions more. Everywhere you looked, you saw evidence that the war had laid its harsh, destructive hands on the town. Onitsha, like most of Biafra, was a marred, disfigured landscape.

Having endured thirty months of a savage war, we had arrived, as it were, on the banks of the future. But even as a child of nine, I could intuit that the future looked every bit as uncertain and ghastly as the horrendous past. I could tell simply by observing my parents' mien.

Onitsha happens to be my mother's birthplace, but I doubt that nativity had anything to do with why we had ended up there. A large town, it drew thousands of refugees. The first wave of arrivals had claimed charred, roofless houses, their walls riddled with bullet holes. Later waves, including us, slept in makeshift tents that dotted the landscape as far as the eye could see. We milled among other refugees, other survivors. We shared the same forlorn countenance, the vacant stares of a befuddled horde. We were animated by the same dreams and hopes. We were driven by the same desperate hunger for food—anything with which to mollify bellies bloated with mere air. All these years later, I still shudder with remembrance of the stink of unwashed bodies. It was a peculiar stench, compounded, I now suspect, by the odour of fear.

In the immediate days after the war, my parents found themselves in the terrible position of owning wands of Biafran currency that had had little value during the war—and were now worthless. By contrast, they did not have a penny in the note that counted: the Nigerian currency. I had always seen my parents as imperturbable, capable of concealing their anxieties. Yet, it was clear to my young eyes that they were grief-stricken. Everybody in that camp shared this communion of grief. Sick, famished and moneyless, how could they negotiate their lives?

The survivors all appeared stunned at the turn of events. They seemed confounded that a cause they took to be just—they *knew* to be irreproachable—could come to such puny, unheralded end. Many had been swayed by what was arguably one of the most extraordinary propaganda campaigns in a war. By the tabulations of the Biafran propaganda machine, we were winning the war. Major reversals were discounted as minor hiccups. Even if they were aware of missteps here and there, many Biafrans had believed that they were well on the path to triumph. And then, next thing, we skidded from intoning the verse of Biafra's indomitability to hearing the drum of "One Nigeria."

One of the major attractions of the Onitsha refugee camp was that it abutted a makeshift barracks for the victorious Nigerian army. Once each day, soldiers distributed relief material—used clothes and blankets as well as tinned food, powdered milk, flour, oats, beans, rice and such like. There was never enough food or clothing to go around. For the refugees, this meant that brawn and grit decided whether you got food or starved. Children, the elderly, the feeble were often pushed to the side, sometimes trampled, in the stampede for scarce food and scarcer blankets. Some days, my father managed to squeak out a few supplies, other days he returned empty-handed. His fluctuating daily fortunes determined whether we ate or went to bed with hunger ringing monstrous bells in our stomachs. On foodless nights, it was impossible to work up enthusiasm about the cessation of war. And then the cry of "Happy survival!" with which refugees greeted one another sounded hollow, a cruel joke.

Despite the hazards, children daily thronged the rowdy food lines. Of course, we had to be wary. We hovered around the edges of the tumult, reluctant to wade into the violent vortex where knuckles, elbows and fists converged – life-and-death calculations that animated the flailing mob.

We hoped that our doleful expressions would invite pity. We had no way of knowing that pity, like sympathy, was a scarce commodity in that arena where everybody was famished.

One day I ventured as, usual, to the raucous food queue. I stood a safe distance away, watching the mayhem in progress from my perch. In the silence of the heart, I prayed that somebody might stir with pity, and then permit me to sneak into the front of the queue for some relief. I was daydreaming when I saw a woman's hand beckoning to me. I shyly went to her. She had a wide, toothy smile, a beautiful specimen.

"What's your name?" she asked.

"Okey," I volunteered, unable to look her in the face.

"Look at me," she commanded gently. I obeyed. "I like your eyes. Will you be my husband?"

I again averted my face, seized by a mixture of flattery, shame and shyness. I was almost ten at the time, old enough to be aware of the woman's beauty, and also of a vague stirring within me. Flattered, ashamed and shy all at once.

"Do you want some food?" she asked.

I answered with the sheerest of nods.

"Wait here."

She went off. I awaited her return, heart pounding, at once expectant and afraid. A few minutes later she handed me a plastic bag filled with beans and a few canned tomatoes. As I thanked her, she said, "Here. Open your hand." Then she dropped ten shillings onto my palm.

I ran to our tent in a flush of exhilaration. I handed the food and coin to my astonished parents, simply reporting that a woman had given them to me. I dared not recount the story of what the philanthropic woman said about my eyes, much less her playful, but intimidating, marital proposal. We had enough food for two or three days. The ten shillings became the first post-war Nigerian coin my family would own.

This story comes back to me each time I learn of yet another war zone, another arena of genocide: Rwanda, Darfur, Kosovo, Liberia, Iraq, Palestine. One is reminded that toxic narratives, oral or written, often precede genocides. These narratives set out to portray the would-be victims, the doomed, the sacrificial lambs marked out for elimination as less than human. As vermin. As stains on the human heritage.

How, then, to combat this scourge of poisonous narratives that fuel genocidal rages? I have been given the tool of fiction, and that's my primary weapon of response. The first step is to look evil in the face and portray it in all its enormity. As Niyi Osundare, a Nigerian poet and friend, has suggested, evil deserves to be made repellently ugly.

Chapter 4

SMALL PEOPLE, BIG WARS: A PERSONAL MEMOIR

Chenjerai Hove

There are the so-called war-poets, but I don't think I am one of them. I happened to be in a place where no one was immune to the whizzing bullets and the brutalities of war. Those years of war, 1976 to 1980, gave me scars and smiles. Scars because real bullets pierced and tore apart the bodies of real women, children and men. Smiles, for, in the midst of death and pain, I saw children, women and men who proudly showed human resilience even in the face of death as they fought for the restoration of their dignity. The colonial rulers had reduced all blacks to the status of third and fourth class citizens as symbolised by coach wagon classifications on the train. Blacks always travelled third or fourth class! Whites, first or second class.

From experience, I have come to wonder if it is true that war breeds poets or that poetry feeds on war. Wherever war has sprung up, poetry too has mushroomed. Maybe we can find out together what it is about war that makes it fertile ground for poetry. Do we, in our poetic lines, cry, even as we celebrate the banalities of death, and the possibilities of life?

When the British poet, Wilfred Owen, wrote his famous "Anthem for Doomed Youth", he did not realise that, as a soldier, he was predicting his own death:

> What passing-bells for these who die as cattle?
> Only the monstrous anger of the guns.
> Only the stuttering rifles' rapid rattle
> Can patter out their hasty orisons.
> No mockeries now for them: no prayers nor bells;
> Nor any voice of mourning save the choirs,
> The shrill, demented choirs of wailing shells;
> And bugles calling for them from sad shires.'
> *(Wilford Owen, "Anthem for Doomed Youth," "googled" from web)*

Owen wrote these lines while in military uniform during World War 1. In short order, he perished like all the other youths he saw "die as cattle" in the slaughterhouses of war amid "the monstrous anger of the guns".

In a war, engulfed by the flames of the war zone, what does a poet do? The choices are at once many and bare.

Nigerian poet Christopher Okigbo took up armour and joined the Biafran War. He too perished, and his death excited many minds and hearts, drenching the whole literary fraternity with new tears. Ali Mazrui wrote a novel, *The Trial of Christopher Okigbo,* in which the narrator puts the poet on trial for abandoning poetry for war, artistic creation for war, finally dying in battle. Mazrui argues that it was not the duty of the poet to make himself cannon fodder instead of cherishing his artistic talent and being an onlooker while his own people "die as cattle."

Our 1986 Nobel luminary, Wole Soyinka, is reputed to have once seized a radio station and forced the broadcaster to play a tape warning the ruling politicians of the peril of announcing false election results. As usual, elections had been rigged and the poet knew the proper results. His thirst for justice forced the poet to abandon the muse for a while in order to write his destiny in other ways and on other different walls. Owen's angry guns had been translated into the "anger" of the armed poet. When Soyinka challenged the Nigerian state's descent into fratricidal war, he was put through months of cruel imprisonment. Soyinka, a poet and a citizen bundled into one being, was under the shadow of death. It is not that the wordsmith had transformed himself into a warmonger!

From 1972 to 1979, the Zimbabwean war of liberation was at its climax. I was in high school in 1972. By 1977, I had graduated from teachers' college, with distinction in Shona language and literature. I did not realise that my real education was about to begin.

After listening to the speeches of the professors and the dry speech of the Rhodesian Secretary for African Education, I was ready to face the world, to teach, to bring light to the African child. Every Sunday afternoon, a famous musical piece aired on the African Service of the Rhodesia Broadcasting Corporation (RBC, now ZBC) to introduce a programme on radio: 'Kudzidza Kwakanaka' (education is glorious). The piece urged Africans/blacks to rush for education as the only beacon of progress.

In his novel, *Waiting for the Rain* (1975), Zimbabwean novelist, Charles Mungoshi, has a character named Lucifer Mandengu. In his pained self-rejection and emotional alienation, the character awakens to the sad realisation that the colonial experience had reduced him to a "geographical and biological error, born here against my will." Lucifer yearns to escape from the countryside of his birth, the God-forsaken rural areas which he is ashamed to call "home."

For Lucifer, education is the conveyor belt that would transport him away from this place he is too ashamed to call home, to a place of salvation and redemption:

> Home.....
> the aftermath of an invisible war
> A heap of dust and rubble
> White immobile heat on the sweltering land
> Home....
> The sharp-nosed vulture
> already smells carrion -
> the ancient woman's skirts
> give off an odour of trapped time
> Home ....
> Return science to its owners
> The witch demands a ransom for your soul
> Your roots claim their rightful pound of clay
> Home...?
> (*Waiting for the Rain*, 1975:52)

During those years of a ruthless war, Zimbabwean novels carried revealing titles:

Waiting for the Rain, Charles Mungoshi, 1975

Coming of the Dry Season, Charles Mungoshi, 1972

House of Hunger, Dambudzo Marechera, 1978

The Unbeliever's Journey, Stanley Nyamufukudza, 1978

A Son of the Soil, Wilson Katiyo, 1977

I took my first teaching post in the southern part of the country that still went by the name of Rhodesia, at Pamushana Secondary School. The backdrop of war was like a nightmare in which you woke up sweating, with the shock of realising that it was, after all, not a nightmare. Life and death stared at me with several, thorny eyes.

The school is located on the side of a massive hill. There is a highway on the northern side, and caves and hills on the southern side. The highway side was as far as the Rhodesian soldiers could go.

Beyond the mountain, there was a no-go area, a "semi-liberated zone," as we called it. It was also a death zone for anyone who dared venture there without permission from "the sons of the soil", the guerrillas. In the caves and the hills that would become our temporary home, we sang and danced to those chimurenga (war) songs which told us that even if death ambushed us, at least we would be free corpses, having died for the restoration of our own dignity.

Then one afternoon, as we sat right there on the mountain top, huge boulders staring at us like hungry soldiers abandoned by their commanders, a local elder affectionately called Mr Shushine, arrived to alert us of the imminent arrival of women carrying baskets of food for the "boys." Young school dropouts ran the information service, surveying the surroundings and reporting back without fail.

Young girls, including my own students, came back from behind the boulders and the caves, giggling in the arms of one or other commander. Looking down the slopes, I saw a chain of women as they painstakingly walked up the steep slope, baskets laden with plates of food balanced on their bare heads.

It was then that I noticed an elderly woman. Bent with age, she walked and crawled up the slope, her load heavy, to come and feed the fighters. Stirred by her determination, I wrote a poem titled "The Way We Fed," in memory of that woman whose name and destiny I would never know:

> Granny forgets the blunt, rapturous pain
> and takes to her load.
> Ah, there! sinewy arms, clawed fingers,
> straps of muscle; and courage.
> Yet an eagle's grip there is.
> She sighs, ancient lips mutter
> some prayer to Nehanda
> and forward she trudges,
> trudging to hope itself - - - but the pain!
> maybe she is late,
> but she suffers not with time,
> time ticks her way
> and she crawls
> like a slave,
> prayerfully
> saintly
> godly forward, heroic as the wind:
> But unheralded by stately choirs,
> Forgotten by national anthem makers!
> (*Up In Arms*, 1982: 12)

What else could a young poet do except to see, record and warn, to witness and tell of the joy and sadness that this search for human dignity evokes?

It was in the midst of this scene that I realised how fragile I was, just as fragile as the old woman, the heroine who will never appear in anybody's national anthem, the one who will die and be buried by the side of a nameless anthill near her old, abandoned homestead. After her death, there would be nothing anymore except faded memories of those who witnessed that tortuous journey.

Without a gun, in times of war, one realises that all is nothing, that those caught in between are nothing. The grass that suffers when two elephants fight, that grass is where poetry resides. Equipped only with words, dreams. What else can the poet do? What does a poet learn? Fragility! Hope in a hopeless situation! Human resilience in a situation where your tomorrow is in other hands over which you have no control. Your fate in another person's loaded gun!

Words become fragile, eggs dropped on a hard rock.

During those years, the bodies of "terrorists" who had been killed were a small number compared to those killed for "assisting" or "running with terrorists." I could have been killed, and my epitaph would have been just like any one of those who had died "running with terrorists." But I was happy to live to celebrate the new meaning of the word "terrorist": one who fights for the liberation of the soil that harbours his/her umbilical cord.

One day I came close to death at the hands of a Rhodesian soldier. When he frantically took aim at me and cocked his gun, I could only look him straight in the eyes. He was sweating. I could already see in his eyes that I was one of those dead "terrs". When the soldier's commander arrived at the nick of time and disarmed him—on discovering that I was the local English master at the school—the soldier's anger boiled still. He warned that I would not survive the night. He would come for me in the secrecy of the night.

During my nocturnal escape, I composed a few lines of a poem called "The Armed Man":

> Look, he is armed,
> the rude gun
> mates with his hunchback
> and his face is armed
> with smoky hate,
> (the flower is withered)

>   that gnaws at inner wells
>   of wild pure hate.
>   He is armed, this man,
>   and his sinews stretch
>   like the hangman's rope
>   as he cowers to the grim gun...
>   (*Up In Arms*, 1982:16)

How else could I, a mere poet, make the reader understand hatred? I decided to focus on his face, on the veins of the armed man, my future assassin.

Statistics have little or no meaning for poets. The individual fate, the tragedy of being trapped in this one place with a would-be assassin, suffice to create the essential metaphor that might make the reader understand the feelings of both victim and victimizer, the armed man and the man who is waiting to die, the hangman wielding his noose, and his victim who wields nothing.

Oh, words, how deficient in meaning! There are events which no poet could name: the mutilated body of a so-called "sell-out", bodies of my students shot and dumped in the river mud, poisoned water flowing in the river so the peasants could drink and all die.

Up in the mountains, the "sell-out" was brought before the "bush tribunal" and found guilty of asking questions about war in the mountains.

The verdict: he had to die. A big bonfire was made on a Sunday afternoon.

Bayonets were brought out, sharp and shiny. The man was sliced slowly, beginning with the ears which were thrown into the fire and roasted for him to eat. A man eating himself!

As he bled to his slow death, one fighter asked him about the taste of his own flesh:

"It is good, but has no salt," the numb, bleeding man said as his arm was chopped off too. And that river of blood flowing out of the human body, that is no stuff for poetry. It is only witness to what war is all about: the burning of all the flowers of human love and compassion.

What can a poet say about such events, such pain? Words have their own limits. I have never written about this incident. All I know is that in war a poet is as fragile as his or her very words. At such moments, human voices are too small to carry the whole burden of human suffering.

At Pamushana, we never taught much. Thursdays to Mondays we were in the mountains. Maybe we would come back Tuesdays. We never knew, and we did not even know that we were still alive.

June 1978, on a Sunday afternoon, the commander, one Shelton Chidoro, calls me aside and warns me that he has a feeling that there could be an ambush. He suggests that the teachers and students should leave. But other commanders refuse. A compromise is reached. Only male teachers should leave. The female teachers and students would remain.

Monday morning, a misty, ominous morning, around 09.00 hours, I am in front of my class, teaching good English. A helicopter lands right in front of my classroom door. A Rhodesian soldier jumps out and orders me to go beyond the mountain to collect the bodies of "the prostitutes of the terrorists," the corpses of my own female students.

I could only stare at the empty chairs of my missing female students, woken to the reality of their death. It would be late afternoon as we ploughed through the undergrowth, putting together the bits of flesh which had been my youthful students. Of this tragedy, I wrote:

> I saw the green leaves
> which swish-shash in stormy days
> to whisper to my sunken heart
> which hops and kicks in me.
> His stench harangued my bowels,
> mixing my nostrils with the long dead
> whose bowels have been embedded
> deep in the glooms of the earth.
> Sure, he died, no doubt.
> Grave-less, ditched, he went...
> (*Up in Arms*, 1982:29)

At the funeral of one of the girls in a nearby village, I could only record poetically the maddening smell of red earth as the grave was dug, and the tears of realising that war takes away words alongside the weak and defenceless. War takes the unarmed and makes them the victims of decisions made by the powerful whose job it is to declare wars but not to fight them.

Small people, big wars!

In times of war, the poet can only dissect, like a surgeon, the small details of what it is to be a victim. The soldiers have no time for that. The politicians have only a vision of power.

In 1978, when we could stand in the same supermarket queue with whites, I was standing behind a pregnant white woman at the till in a shop. Without intending to do so, her fingers brought out a loaded revolver from her purse. She looked at it, cast a wink at me, and returned the revolver where it came from. A few days later, I was imagining what it was for a woman to carry a gun in her handbag, alongside the cash. I knew that young as she was, her young husband was probably on military call-up. Poetic lines came to my pen, searching for her emotions:

> This war!
> I am tired
> of a husband who never sleeps
> guarding the home or on call-up,
> Never sleeping.
> Maybe inside him he says
> 'I am tired of a wife
> who never dies
> so I can stop guarding.'
> (*Up In Arms*, 1982: 9)

We were victims, she and I. She was as much a victim as I, forced to carry a gun instead of flowers. And to think that Rhodesia at that time had the world record for divorces and suicides among the white population! While they carried guns and sang "Rhodesians Never Die," they were already dead inside, their lives shattered by what Bruce Moore-King, an ex-Rhodesian soldier, reminiscently described in his memoirs as "a war that was a glorious adventure, an easy test of manhood, a war that was right and always honourable, a war where the good were white and the evil were black, a war as simple as that." (*White Man, Black War*, 1988:3)

At the same time the pregnant white woman carried a revolver in her handbag, my own wife was also pregnant. I wrote a poem titled 'A War-Time Wife' in which I tried to visualise what it was like to be pregnant in a time of war:

> ...Till one day, maybe night
> raids rupture hope in expectancy:
> Fertility perishing in thatched graves
> to drive lead-like tears
> Down slippery times
> and swallowed by history's gorgons.'
> (*Up In Arms*, 1982: 10)

Wars may end, but the victims refuse to go away. They haunt me, like a shadow that waits for me at sunset, besides me, my eternal friend ready to go even into the grave with me.

Many years later, when the war had ended and people still sang songs glorifying battles which they had not even seen, I wrote of one of the remnants of the victims of war, Johana's mother, in my novel, *Shadows*. After her husband is killed in a civil war that she does not understand, she tries to get government help to bring up her few remaining children. But everywhere she went, she finds out "No one knows Johana's father...Johana's mother hears the echoes of the new lullabies from the lips of the mothers carrying silent children. She hears them sing about the red moon is blood, the eye of the bull is a bullet, the girl's long neck is a needle. She hears it all in the silence of this house of death where life would have to start anew, like the dead leaves that would have to rise again from their death." (*Shadows*, 1991:108)

War and violence create new images and metaphors in the heart of the writer, the poet. Through war, a new language is created in all its beauty and ugliness. War creates new ways of mourning, new ways of searching for that which makes human beings sad. Above all, it is the vulnerability of all that surfaces and reminds the writer that the only task left for words is to dissect the sorrow, pain and sadness which can come from the human heart in times of war. At the same time, the poet celebrates the capacity of human beings to develop a new form of human endurance and resilience, the capacity to hope.

References & Recommended Reading

Hove, Chenjerai (1982), *Up In Arms*. Harare: Zimbabwe Publishing House.

Hove, Chenjerai (1985), *Red Hills of Home*, Gweru, Mambo Press.

Hove, Chenjerai (1986), *Masimba Evanhu (People's Power?)*, Gweru, Mambo Press.

Hove, Chenjerai (1988), *Bones*. Harare: Baobab Books.

Hove, Chenjerai. (1991), *Shadows*. Harare: Baobab Books.

Hove, Chenjerai (1998), *Rainbows in the Dust*. Harare: Baobab Books.

Hove, Chenjerai (2002), *Palaver Finish*. Harare: Weaver Press.

Moore-King, Bruce (1988), *White Man, Black War*. Harare, Baobab Books.

Mungoshi, Charles (1975), *Waiting for the Rain*: Oxford, Heinemann.

Owen, Wilfred (1918), "Anthem to Doomed Youth" (www.google.com)

Mazrui, Ali (1971), *The Trial of Christopher Okigbo*. Oxford, Heinemann.

Soyinka, Wole (2006), *You Must Set Forth at Dawn: A Memoir*. New York, Random House.

Chapter 5

WAR AND THE WRITTEN WORD

Juliane Okot Bitek

Writing about war is a life affirming act. I first started writing about war as an eleven year-old who was frustrated about the difficulties that the post-Idi Amin government in Uganda had in uniting the different factions. *Why can't we just divide the country into three?* My plaintive cry was a source of much amusement for the adults, but it made sense in my girlish mind. We were five siblings who had to share things, divide up things and give up things. I suppose I was advocating for a federal state – divide and share – but I had no idea that the adult world functions a lot differently from the one I was familiar with. What I was after at the time is what propels me to continue to write on war – that there is life after *this*. There are better times ahead, and that we will survive this one, too.

War comes at us from different angles. We are bombarded with it by reporters who report from the battlefields; by the politicians who declare war on drugs, terror, corruption, hunger, poverty and pollution; by the well-intentioned health authorities who declare war on diseases like cancer, malaria and HIV/AIDS. We see the risen dust behind a bullet-proofed reporter whose hair flies in the wind, who is hoarse from trying to be a voice from mayhem and a place of death and destruction. The imperative to take the images from the war front to the television sets is a brave attempt to link the warm and safe spaces where the television sets light up with the world that is dimmed by bombs and lost lives.

We are connected. We are all connected. Africans, living and writing from the Diaspora, feel it even more so when we read and write about the situations at home where there is little we can do. We can write. And in the moment of expression we delve right back to times when things were not as they are now. We recall, and we know of, better times. Better times, not always measured in economic comfort, but times when there was easy laughter and children's voices in the compound. We wish to recuperate those voices and write them back into existence. Writing is an attempt to separate those memories from the gunk that is war. As a teenager, I watched a woman soldier in combat with a baby tied on her back, firing a machine gun into a crowd. The moment is crystallized in the panic that I had, not for the crowd that was dispersing in terror, but for the baby on her back. Suppose someone shot her baby?

Until then, I had never considered that mothers could be armed soldiers. I had never considered that armed soldiers were fathers, brothers, sisters, aunts, uncles, friends, lovers, cousins, neighbors, and likely grandparents. My maternal uncle was a soldier. My own soldier brother was killed in action. My brother died young, handsome and fiercely passionate about his young wife, daughter and his family. We were heart sick when he died. Keny was my brother before he was a soldier, and I never thought of him as a person hired to shoot and kill. That was before the woman with a baby on her back aimed at a crowd of people, all somebody's somebody, all loved. I stood on the balcony of The Centre overlooking Kampala Road and did not think about the irony of watching a mother-killer. In those days, I wrote of teenage angst and budding love. Not war. But that memory was seared in my mind. I think about it as the moment I realized that we are all casualties of war. We who watch the action as if from afar are as touched as we who shoot, are shot at, who die, who are separated by years of memory, or remain tied tightly against our mother's back. So we etch our memories in marks that represent feelings, places, reasons, a prayer and a plea for it to come to an end.

The war rages on, in contemporary times as it did in the past. We could turn off the radio, change the channel on TV, shrug our shoulders – *that's their problem; people never learn.* But the images continue to haunt us as children affected by war stare out with empty eyes, out from the inside pages of major newspapers, since there's no space for them in the front page.

We might send money, less than a dollar a day, to help these hapless victims, as they are tagged. We might walk in solidarity, mimicking the night commuter children of Acholi, sending awareness to those others: that we know, we are watching, we care about those other people. At the end of the day, the money is siphoned off to wherever it ends up, and the walk ends, but the fighting does not. And neither does the misery of war.

So we write about that experience which holds us hostage to ineffectiveness and powerlessness. There is a kinship established by walkers and the donors which only lasts as long as the act of giving and walking. After, we go back home to the pangs of pain we hold in our hearts. That is a place that is especially lonely when it is your home that has been placed on the map by the insecurity and the incredulity of night commuter children, child soldiers and sex slaves. The first degree of connection belongs to us who are related by blood, kinship, neighborhood, friendship, and the singular planet on which we all live. Therein lie the responsibility and the reason why we cannot be comfortable with war.

When I read about people being forced to sit on charcoal stoves by soldiers in Iris Chang's *Rape of Nanking*, I know that I had seen the same thing in 1985 when soldiers burst into our kitchen dragging a man who was crying and pleading for his life. One soldier ordered us to take the food off the stove while the other forced the prisoner to sit on the fiery charcoal stove at gun point. The man's screams did not impress the soldiers who made us watch the tortured man's tears rain down his face.

Chang's rendition of the Second World War in Nanking, China at the hands of the Japanese brought that memory back painfully, but necessarily. Because, as she says, forgetting means that we are bound to war again. Being a witness imbues us with a special responsibility – to record and reveal what is hidden. And so we write. Iris Chang wrote as a witness to her grandparents' generation. She revived the nightmare of Nanking in an act of memorialization and consecrated memory. We must never forget Nanking. She made her mark and left the legacy of her grandparents' experience that was nearly non-existent, having not been written down.

Iris Chang is dead now, but her words live and we cannot forget Nanking. We see our lives reflected in that war and other wars worldwide and over time. It connects us and propels us to recognize ourselves in the other because we are the other, even we, the witnesses who decide that we have seen enough and change channels.

Shutting off the information does not distance us from the immediacy of the war even if we are too far to smell the burning flesh or to hear the cries of a grown man pleading for his life. It presents itself, like a secret that refuses to stay hidden. The frustration and impatience of the channel changers meet in the inside pages of the major newspapers, or in the front page headlines where places of war are also places that could determine the price of war which the western economy depends on. And so it touches every family out here. There is no getting away from it, and so we write. We write to relay the inescapability of the situation that might seem so far removed, but really cannot be any closer. We write to say these places, these people, these times are also places, times, and spaces that were once inhabited by laughter and the footsteps of children pattering about in the yard.

As I write, my own home of northern Uganda has recently experienced a lull while the Lord's Resistance Army (LRA) and the government of Uganda hammer out a peace agreement. The lull is like a long sigh. It is a sigh of relief, but a sigh nevertheless. This could be a good thing. It is a good thing, but we continue to hold our breath as we look around at the devastation, the trauma and the hidden landmines, like the ache of a pimple before it surfaces to mar the landscape and the life and limb of whoever touches upon it.

This is where my parents and grandparents were born. This is the place that holds fond childhood memories, passed on to me, a child born in exile. I learned about different kinds of mangos and the smell of seasonal fires in the dry season. I learned about a grandmother who would not continue primary school because she wanted to dance and had heard that only prostitutes went to school.

My mother tells me about how her own great-grandmother was struck down in a hail of bullets with a child in her arms, at the turn of the century, leaving her grandmother motherless. She doesn't know what war it was, only that every time her grandmother picked up the last grain of rice from the floor she claimed it was because she grew up as a child without a mother. The armed mother shooting into a crowd reveals herself in a myriad of ways. She shoots, she scores. Perhaps her child still lives. My great-grandmother's baby brother did not.

My sense of happiness begins in Acholi-land and the knowledge that my parents and grandparents grew up in a place of peace, fertile soil, dance, poetry and music. I carry this information like a gem in my body. The stories I gleaned from my parents and their home makes me smile, makes me laugh out loud, makes me sure that the world as it is has not always been a miserable place that can be shut off by the change of a channel and the bitterness that this knowledge lodges at the back of the throat. We walk for peace, for the environment, for cancer, AIDS, and against the torture of prisoners everywhere. As we walk, we exchange brief greetings and stories with strangers and sometimes exchange phone numbers and email addresses to strengthen our solidarity. Islands of good times make themselves known in demonstrations. But our footsteps remain in the dirt beneath our feet as we carry our indignation through the streets, holding placards, screaming into megaphones because we live in the part of the world where we can, never hesitating to ask: what is it that we can do? What is it that we do that can change anything?

Writers write. They write because they, too, can. They write even when they should not, even when they are incarcerated, as Wole Soyinka and Ngugi wa Thiongo were because they wrote. Writers write, possibly because if they don't the words will gather up in their throats and suffocate them in their sleep. So they write. I write because the act of writing keeps me in conversation with others who write to maintain our being in existence. We write to aggravate those who believe that they can silence us by killing us, by snuffing our lives out. I write to prove that war is no Medusa and I am not paralyzed, even though the horror often leaves me speechless. Perhaps they will go on to declare war on words, on literature, on writers – as the government of Kenya once did against wa Thiongo's *Matigari*. Or as the government of Uganda did against his friend, Okot p'Bitek, which resulted in some of his children being born in exile, away from a home that is still unwaveringly bright in their hearts. War against the written word and the writers who write them, is one that cannot be fought and won. Once written into existence, words cannot be unwritten. They can be erased, burned and censored, but that will have to be after having been written into existence. And having been, and been read, is reason enough to think about, remember and pass on.

Chapter 6

THE NIGERIAN WRITER AND THE NIGER DELTA CRISIS

Ogaga Ifowodo

Nearly half a century ago, a high profile meeting of African writers was held in Stockholm. The theme was: 'The Future of African Literature.' I am remembering the famous Afro-Scandinivian Writers' Conference of 1960. Writers were quick to locate the dilemma Africa faced in the immediate aftermath of independence. One of the participants at that conference, Wole Soyinka, twenty-six years away from the Nobel Prize in literature, discerned the African writer's major failure as his turning away from vision, and so from his historical role as the "special eye and ear" of his society.

Soyinka's contribution entitled "The Writer in a Modern African State" has since gone down as a classic assessment of the nascent African literature of the decade of independence. But it remains valuable even now for its insights on the role of the writer in an even more troubled Africa in the epoch of globalisation and neo-liberal corporate governance. To Soyinka in 1960, the writer's sensitivity to mood, and so to the needs of his people which in the numinous moment of independence demanded a "pooling together of every mental resource," may have led him to suspend the "unique reflection on experience and events" that alone define him as a writer.

When European publishers, in the service of an outside world whose "curiosity far exceeded its critical faculties", arrived on the scene to create an added distraction from vision, from "the ever-present fertile reality," the stage was set for a cession of the sceptre of vision to the politician. Inevitably, the writer failed to address the palpable situation of a continent twice raped and devastated — by slavery and colonialism — with the required degree of critical reflection. This is what led Soyinka to his controversial declaration:

"The average published writer in the few years of the post-colonial era was the most celebrated skin of inconsequence to obscure the true flesh of the African dilemma."

As we know, this failing would be redressed with a vengeance in the period of post-independence disillusionment. The very best works of this era burned with rage and seethed with despair at the phenomenal squandering of material and spiritual riches by the politicians who took the reins of power from the European colonisers. From Soyinka's own *Madmen and Specialists* to Ayi Kwei Armah's *The Beautyful Ones Are Not Yet Born* and Cheikh Hamidou Kane's *Ambiguous Adventure* — just to name a few — the African writer was fully in his element as visionary and primal interpreter of his society, as the keeper of its conscience. In short, "Reality, the ever-present fertile reality" constituted almost wholly the angst-ridden horizon of his Muse.

What then is the reality of the African writer *today*? We can sum it up in a few crises so horrendous they are known just by the names of the bloodied patches of the continent where they shamed their land and shocked the world: Liberia, Somalia, Rwanda, Sierra Leone, Darfur, the Niger Delta — again, just to name a few. The trail of blood and tears and sighs that chronicles these and the numerous unnamed crises is given further reach today by the power of instant journalism, replete with gruesome images repeated in the fifteen-minute bulletins of cable and satellite television.

With the judicial murder in 1995 of the writer and activist, Ken Saro-Wiwa, and his eight Ogoni compatriots, the Niger Delta crisis of Nigeria made its entry onto the list of atrocities that would justify the charge of a universal abandonment of our humanity. For, lest it be forgotten, the murders took place just as Britain and its erstwhile colonies smugly urged restraint and diplomacy in order to appease a military tyrant, the late General Sani Abacha, in the hope that he would then be pleased to halt his hangman already at the gallows.

Since we will all know, I expect, of the atrocities closer home to us in our respective corners of the continent, let me now devote the remaining part of this chapter to the one that is a *lived* reality for me: Nigeria's Niger Delta. And I do so, first, for the reason underscored by my italics in the preceding sentence, and, second, for the reason that the Niger Delta crisis has rightly to be seen as a national allegory.

If the story of Nigeria is at once the nightmarish case of failure of vision worsened by a profligate squandering of promise and hope, then Saro-Wiwa's precursor was the first to understand the Niger Delta crisis as the national tragedy miniaturised.

Activist Isaac Adaka Boro was aware of the role oil — first palm oil and later crude oil — had come to play in Nigerian politics from the days of the Royal Niger Company's colonial monopoly of trade to the Royal/Dutch Shell's commanding place in the oil and gas sector of Nigeria's monocultural economy. He was dead on the point when he saw the Niger Delta as "the booty" of the emergent nation's rulers. Boro's "twelve-day revolution" was sparked by the fear of being "throw[n] ... into perpetual slavery" in the wake of Nigeria's first military putsch of January 1966. Although he would gain reprieve and fight on the federal side during the Biafran War of 1967-70 that eventually claimed his life, the irony is that Boro, like all inhabitants of the Niger Delta, have been caught since the colonial suzerainty of Lord Lugard between a rock and ... well, the deep blue sea.

And what the Nigerian writer is in danger of doing is succumbing to a purblind vision defined by an unbroken cycle of politicians and militricians insistent on reserving for itself the right to name and condemn resistant inhabitants of the delta as "saboteurs" and "criminals" fit for the gallows or the army's bullets while they, the booty-hunters-in-power, are statesmen. And in the process, ceding the grounds of the ethical battle for the nation to insurgents.

As shown by the Breaking News section of *The Guardian* online of Friday, 17 February 2006, which had the report, "Militant group declares 'total war' warning;" the report was short but had, nevertheless, all the ingredients for a full story:

> "A militant commander in the oil-rich southern Niger Delta has told the BBC his group is declaring "total war" on all foreign oil interests. The Movement for the Emancipation of the Niger Delta has given oil companies and their employees until midnight on Friday night to leave the region. It recently blew up two oil pipelines, held four foreign oil workers hostage and sabotaged two major oilfields. The group wants greater control of the oil wealth produced on their land. It is the first time the military leader of the Mend movement, Major-General Godswill Tamuno, has spoken publicly of his group's aims. ... He told the BBC ... that they had launched their campaign, called "dark February" to ensure that all foreign oil interests left. He said that they had had enough of the exploitation of their resources and wanted to take total control of the area to get their fair share of the wealth."

I have quoted this "manifesto" at length because, short as it is, and relayed through the filter of two news media — BBC and *The Guardian* — it, nonetheless, defines MEND as a resistance group, one of many in the Niger Delta, resisting a brutish and arrogant exploitation by the Nigerian state. Put in other words, what Nigeria's former governor of Oyo State in the so-called Second Republic, and later minister of justice under General Olusegun Obasanjo, the assassinated Bola Ige, described as Nigeria "stealing from the Niger Delta." All with the attendant environmental devastation of the region as the salt the oil companies rub in the Delta inhabitants' injuries. It also highlights the demand for ownership and greater control of the resources bestowed on their land. As is clear to all but those who will not give up stealing from the Niger Delta, resource control is another name for the derivation principle which ought to be a given in a federal republic. It is not a principle unknown to Nigeria's efforts at constitutionalism as earlier and better constitutions than the military-imposed books of expropriation that go by the name of the 1979 and 1989 constitutions, duly recognised. It ensures that first 100, and later, 50 percent, of national revenue went to the regions. It is not only an ethical principle, but one that is politically and economically unimpeachable. The rest of Nigeria, as late as the 2005 national constitution review conference convened by Obasanjo, thinks, however, that 17 percent is more than enough.

The reason for this outrage is clear: oil, together with its accompanying natural gas, is located exclusively in the Niger Delta peopled by ethnic minorities. Were it located in any other part of the country, or were the economy dependent on cotton, or groundnuts, or cocoa, resource control would be holy writ, enshrined in any constitution and protected against easy amendments like Obasanjo's Land Use Decree, later an Act, of 1978.

The cynicism — and more about this word soon — that underlies the brutal national conspiracy to lay the delta to waste, to deny it the benefit of the resources nature endowed it with for the sustenance of its people, was propounded with blood-curdling indifference by Chief Philip Asiodu, a former Nigerian 'super' permanent secretary. 'Super' permanent secretaries, I should let the reader know, were the powers-behind-the-military throne of General Yakubu Gowon, (1966 – 1975) and chief prosecutor of the Biafran War of 1967-1970. As well-trained bureaucrats, they were the principal policy-makers and executors increasingly deferred to by a young and inexperienced Jack Gowon and his Supreme Military Council of soldiers who knew little or nothing about governance, not trained to govern, and lacking experience or a national tradition in that respect.

Asiodu, in a lecture he gave to public servants in 1980, sought, at first, to hide his hand by trying to justify the inhuman policy of the exploitation he championed. So he spoke about the "inhospitable" type of terrain all over the world where crude oil is likely to be found; why, as a result of this topographical fact, a "massive injection of money" would be required to bring the Niger Delta up to liveable standards comparable to the rest of the country. Continuing on this deceptive trail, Asiodu tried to present himself as not merely out for the oil by any means by showing a slight appreciation of the delta people's grievance. He said:

> "oil-producing areas ... see themselves as losing non-replaceable resources while replaceable resources of agriculture and industry are being developed elsewhere largely with oil revenue."

But that was all the selflessness, all the statesmanship, and all the commitment to equity, justice and fair play the erudite public servant could muster. Without any qualms about the glaring *non sequitur*, Asiodu then proposed as follows:

> "Given, however, the small size and population of the oil-producing area, it is not cynical to observe that even if the resentments ... continue, they cannot threaten the stability of the country nor affect continued economic development."

Not cynical? No doubt, the population of a people determines what is cynical — especially if vital resources happen to be buried under their soil. What we have in Nigeria's Niger Delta, then, is a long-standing official policy of the expendability of the human beings that populate it and under whose feet lie the oil and gas that power the country.

If you look at it carefully, you will see the blueprint of ethnic cleansing or genocide:

> "Given their small size ... they cannot threaten the stability of the country nor affect continued economic development."

What if they do? As, indeed, they have to some degree, beginning in 1993? We all know what happened during the subsequent military occupation of Ogoniland, and, indeed, the militarization of the entire Niger Delta. The mayhem visited on the region has left permanent scars in too many towns and villages razed or flattened to the ground.

It suffices, I think, that the military expedition sent by General Obasanjo to Odi in 1999 proves just how alive and well this policy of pacification, and if necessary, elimination, of the people of the Niger Delta, is in Nigeria's corridors of power.

I have tried to capture the dismal reality of this land and people in my last volume of poetry, *The Oil Lamp*, which is one long poem in five sections. In Part IV of the book, you will find a close resemblance to Chief Asiodu in a nameless character talking about the official dispossession of a people in the dullest tones of bureaucratic double-speak.

To return to my thoughts, the MEND statement had forewarned of coming acts of rebellion; yet I was unsure how to react to the news that nine new hostages had been taken. Nor was I sure of my feelings about the sabotage of an oil terminal belonging to Shell, even though I have long held the view that rather than the inhabitants of the Niger Delta letting their oil continue to be hemlock to them but "milk and honey" to the thieving ruling elite and its foreign collaborators, they should ensure it remains in the ground. I must report, though, that when I finally decided I could applaud the recent acts of desperation, I found comfort in the words of that great anti-colonial revolutionary thinker, Frantz Fanon, pronounced in *The Wretched of the Earth*, his classic study of the violence of colonialism and of an insensitive post-independence petit-bourgeoisie:

> "As for we who have decided to break the back of colonialism, our historic mission is to sanction all revolts, all desperate actions, all those abortive attempts drowned in rivers of blood."

For "colonialism," you need only substitute the internal colonialism of successive Nigerian governments and the existing practice and effects of neo-colonialism.

The Nigerian government, it would seem, also understands the Fanonian creed, even if unwittingly. The freed hostages are from the United States, the United Kingdom, Bulgaria and Honduras. Among the new hostages are three Americans and one Briton. The immediate grouse of MEND is the series of aerial bombardments of Ijaw villages soon after the four hostages were released. The bombardments were carried out by Brigadier Elias Zamani, commander of the Joint Military Task Force set up by General Obasanjo's federal government to secure the Niger Delta for uninterrupted oil exploration.

To every right thinking person, Brigadier Zamani's sorties were nothing but reprisal acts by the federal government aimed at intimidating the Niger Delta communities. Zamani, however, claims to have been throwing his bombs at illegal oil bunkerers. His targets were "defenceless" villagers, one of whom bemoaned his fate thus:

> "How can you explain to your defenceless and law-abiding aged parents that your community is being attacked because you complained of underdevelopment?"

Then it is either that Zamani is a liar, a bad soldier and officer undeserving of his rank and post, or oil bunkering could ever be a villager's undertaking. As for the latter, all the evidence points to oil-bunkering being essentially beyond the economy or competence of such simple villagers as inhabit the creeks of the Niger Delta. The illegal operation is simply too sophisticated and requires too heavy a capital outlay. The evidence, in fact, points to generals and other rich and powerful men, well connected to government, colluding with foreign oil pirates linked to criminal international oil rings. If locals are involved in the act at all, it must be at a very low level. What is more, they will have to be latecomers to the very lucrative, but high-risk undertaking. Even then, they must have the protection of powerful men in government and in the security services for any chance of success.

Oil being the heart and soul of Nigeria, the *raison d'être* of the nation, every government pays the closest attention to it. We can add to this point the recent declaration of the Gulf of Guinea as a strategic area of interest by the United States for the simple reason that it considers oil a security question. The two wars against Iraq make this view clear enough, if any proof were needed! The U.S. government has been arming the Nigerian state for even more effective pacification of the Delta.

So, whomever we choose to believe — the general or the villager — it remains debatable whether aerial bombardment is the best way to deal with an internal economic menace.

But no one has accused General Obasanjo and Nigeria's greedy and callous ruling elite of ever letting the thought of the best way to deal with the crisis of nationhood that currently shakes the country to its very foundations pass fleetingly through their minds. Since MOSOP and Ken Saro-Wiwa marked the dawn of a new consciousness in the Niger Delta, even succeeding in halting oil exploitation by the powerful Shell in Ogoniland, the methods for pacifying the 'primitive tribes' of that hapless region have been eerily similar. Just one parallel will do. Brigadier Zamani's JTF is only a clone of Major (later promoted Colonel) Paul Okuntimo's Rivers State Internal Security Task Force. Major Okuntimo is the Major Kitemo, aka, Kill-Them-All, who meets his nemeses in simple unarmed villagers in Part III of *The Oil Lamp*.

Subterfuge, bombs, bullets, torture, and when all that failed, judicial murder by hanging, have been staples of the dispossession strategy. So, if in the matter of foreign hostages, Obasanjo has been willing to negotiate first and send in the bomb squad after their release, it is only in order to ensure he would not deliver corpses to George W. Bush and Tony Blair. Otherwise, his only option would surely have been the punitive expedition — like the one he sent to Odi just six months into his first term.

The question that arises for General Obasanjo, or whoever may succeed him, as president of the republic is: how many more times is he prepared to negotiate the freedom of foreign hostages and then send the bomb squad after? What happens when the inevitable occurs; when, feeling too weakened by such negotiations, he calls their bluff and launches a show of strength, thereby driving the hostage-takers to the further act of desperation: killing a hostage or two? How much longer before he throws a military cordon around the entire Niger Delta? And when he thus elevates the current low-intensity warfare to an open shooting war, how prepared is he for what that means for the purported national unity at whose altar he is willing to sacrifice justice?

There are, of course, many more questions to ask a president who can turn two confessions of being an accomplice after the fact of the treasonable felony of election rigging into a joke; whose overt or covert actions stoke the fires of a national impeachment frenzy threatening the stability of the nation on the eve of his departure from office; an anti-corruption president and former chairman of Transparency International who, apparently, does not know what it means to abuse office, nor that whether unearned gifts are solicited or unsolicited, their recipient is as tainted as their corrupt giver.

The final question is: how much longer will he deny the nation the only viable chance of bringing itself from the precipice of self-destruction by way of a sovereign national conference — or any gathering of the people however styled for the purpose of fashioning a nation for themselves, but with indubitable plenary powers? MEND is an interesting acronym, indeed, given our times. And it comes to freshen the writing on the wall which says to Nigeria's obdurate president and the tiny but vicious clique of nation-wreckers, Mend your ways or time will inevitably mend the nation with or without you.

And if the writer in Nigeria is not to find himself sewn up in the most *uncelebrated* "skin of inconsequence" to obscure the prurient flesh of the Nigerian dilemma — which the world also reads rightly as a continental allegory — then he must, even against the desultory feeling of merely pouring words on troubled waters, return to the upward path of making the inescapable truths of his society the central elements of his vision. That alone will help to end the continent's unending cycle of dehumanising crises and at the same time make him answer without shame or remorse to the appellation: writer.

Chapter 7

A LIZARD GROWS ANOTHER TAIL: THE PERSISTENCE OF WAR IN MY WRITING

Thabisani Ndlovu

I suspect that if I had not been a "child of war," I would not have become a writer. I was between the ages of six and twelve when some of the bloodiest conflicts raged in Zimbabwe. This period spans the height of the liberation war in 1978, the clash between Robert Mugabe's Zimbabwe African National Liberation Army (ZANLA) and the Joshua Nkomo-led Zimbabwe People's Revolutionary Army (ZIPRA) in November 1980 and February 1981 at Entumbane where our family town house was. This period was closely followed by the Gukurahundi (literally "the early rain that washes away the chaff before the spring rains") onslaught, a state perpetrated violence against defenceless citizens in Matabeleland. More than twenty thousand people were systematically massacred by the Korean-trained Fifth Brigade. This was done under the pretext of quelling dissidents. My rural home of Lupane was one of the most badly affected places.

Before I reached adolescence I had started making sense of the madness. It was in the running and hiding and savage beatings. I heard about people being burnt alive. I saw corpses – the inevitable harvest of war – ever before I became an adolescent. My mother shattered moments of calm by talking incessantly to other adults about the war and Gukurahundi. I relived some incidents, and had fresh ones planted in my mind through my mother's narratives of the war. She has a most impressive command of the Ndebele language and her strength lies in creating graphic images. In fact, some of the sharp imagery in my writing comes from her.

In 1993, my short story titled "The Bhudis" won fourth prize in the Modus Publications short story competition. It is a story about the violence of the guerillas, the freedom fighters, the "Bhudis," our "brothers" as they preferred to be called, on defenceless civilians during the height of Zimbabwe's liberation struggle. The story is told from a child's point of view. This particular story would set a precedent for my future subject matter and narrative technique. In 2005, I had two stories, "Heads and Tails" and "Kristina," both narrated from a child's perspective, published in *Creatures Great and Small*, edited by Jairos Kangira. "Heads and Tails" is a "war" story in the sense that, although the action takes place immediately after the cease fire, the story focuses on four boys, one of whom has recently had his father arrested for killing a fellow villager who had got his mother killed by guerillas during the war. In 2006, "The Boy With A Crooked Head" was published in *Short Writings from Bulawayo III*, edited by Jane Morris. It, like the other stories mentioned above, is told from a child's point of view but a somewhat mentally unstable child. The story focuses on the disappearance of the boy's uncle during the Gukurahundi period. In 2008, "Stampede" was published in *Long Time Coming: Short Writings from Zimbabwe*, edited by Jane Morris. The main character is a soldier in a "never ending war in peace time" (134).

Most of the incidents in the four short stories to be discussed here are informed by real life events either as I recall them or as told by my mother, or other people. In fact, the stories are an amalgam of all these sources, refracted through my imaginative manipulation of setting and characters. There were also the aftermaths. There were literally visible scars of war-related incidents on people's bodies, people who had been disabled by the violence – amputated limbs, missing ears and other parts of the body that had been cut off. There were also the invisible scars – the psychological trauma of having been violated and humiliated. Above all, there was the conspicuous absence of those who had died. In a sense, my subject had already been chosen for me – and maybe the point of view as well. I have learnt many writing lessons from representing violence and using the first person child's point of view. I look at these four stories and see an incremental psychological formation that parallels a sharpening writing technique. Needless to say the whole exercise has helped me deal with my own psychological trauma.

In 1993 my mother had a chance encounter with one of the guerillas who had been a terror during the war. The man had nearly wiped out our whole family before the timely intervention of another guerilla group that overturned his decision. For days, Mother would not stop verbally attacking the man. She detailed his acts of brutality. She spoke about how, on that day of narrow escape, the man had been bent on slitting open Mother's tummy. She was seven months pregnant by then. So it was in 1993, the year I would turn twenty-two and was a second year university student, that I openly engaged my mother, probing for circumstance and motive. Some of it made sense. The result was a rush of memories I thought I had safely shelved away or destroyed completely. I started ferreting for cause and effect in the events I could remember. I felt the urge to put down those stories. There were two reasons. First, because I could, for the first time, see several motives and how these tended to clash. I had also read somewhere that writing was a therapeutic exercise. In short, for the first time I thought I could master my memories of violence. They were less frightening because they made sense and they were now peopled with human beings with different aims and desires. With hindsight, I think it is almost impossible to write about horrific events until one can make sense of what was fuelling the whole macabre drama. I also think by vocalizing some of the experiences, my mother was in her way attempting to understand the whole episode. I detested my mother's almost obsessive talk about war and the Gukurahundi then, just as I was embarrassed by her loud voice and laughter. Today I'm glad she passed on those narratives for me to transform and share with the rest of the world.

I had written stories before "The Bhudis." Most of them were "love" stories – the love-struck boy who will die for his lover, lovers who part momentarily only to "belong together forever," or the man who jumps out of the window when the cuckolded husband unexpectedly comes back home and so on. But how would I represent heinous acts of brutality?

My first attempt at a war story was in third person narrative. I wanted a child or children to be focalized in the story. From my high school readings of literature I had learnt of the fragility and innocence of children through Blake and Wordsworth. From the same high school course, I knew from Dickens (*Dombey and Son* and *Oliver Twist*) that a child can be used as an evocative literary device, as a vehicle for social commentary and reform. So, I wanted my readers to see the evil of the perpetrators of violence and be filled with both horror and indignation. In my first attempt, guerillas kill people on suspicion that they gave information to Ian Smith's army and one of the women suspected of having an affair with a soldier from the Rhodesian forces is ordered to put her little baby inside a mortar and pound him with a pestle. Several babies are chased around and bayoneted. I had to write that, I thought, because although I had not witnessed the pounding of the baby in the mortar, it had happened and Mother never missed an opportunity to mention that incident. Here were children denied the frolicsome liberty of childhood as evinced in Blake's poetry. I went a step further. I would put Blake to shame, with his sooty children sweeping chimneys and complaining that the inside of a church is very cold. Here were children being killed for sport, alongside their parents. This was serious stuff. Every page of that story is be-spattered with blood. I was sure my readers would be shocked and outraged.

I tried to find myself in this gory story. Was I one of the children who had been killed? I realized that to insert myself in the narrative, I should survive to tell the tale. So, I tried the same story from a first person point of view. The story quickly got emotionally heavy and I got bogged down by too much detail. There were so many things I wanted to say. I remembered from my mother's narrative the numerous motives and plans of characters. How would I represent the jealous neighbour? The sadistic and lascivious guerilla torturing a woman because *he* could not have her that day? Or how would a child process all this? I could not finish the story, no matter how many times I went back to it.

By chance I attended a creative writing soiree chaired by Chenjerai Hove who was then writer-in-residence at the University of Zimbabwe. I also met a student who had enjoyed Luis Bernado Honwana's *We Killed Mangy Dog* (1969). This was Memory Chirere, who is now a successful writer in both Shona and English. Chirere lent me Honwana's book. It was stunning. The stories are so simple yet captivating. When I started seeing a subtext of meaning in each of those stories, I knew that they are deceptively simple (what, I would later learn, is called understatement). I thought I now knew how to narrate my story in a way that would reveal characters' motives. I also happened to read Charles Mungoshi's *Coming of the Dry Season* (1972) a couple of weeks after reading *We Killed Mangy Dog*. It was as if I had been waiting for something to click the right way in my head. But these two writers were not writing about the kind of violence I knew, the kind I wanted to forget.

Then I saw the Modus Publications advertisement calling for short stories. I needed the prize money more than the recognition as a writer. As the submission deadline drew nearer, I found myself writing what was to become "The Bhudis." I first went back to my earlier efforts on the same story. After the Honwana and Mungoshi experience, the over-dramatization of violence became glaring. I tried to write the story and got stuck again. But how could it be when these events had happened and I had recently read some books I thought had unlocked my dilemma? I felt cheated and embarrassed. I was disappointed with the power of the written word. It could never capture my experiences. I would never submit any piece and I would never get that prize money. Reluctantly, I attended another reading and writing discussion. You could start a story from the end, was the focus. I knew that. It sounded so trite.

The Modus Publications deadline was fast approaching. I started the story from the end, the consequence of the violence. I wrote that story in one sitting. All the time I was mindful of the lessons I had learnt from Honwana and Mungoshi in handling a child's point of view – that a child's world is essentially one of sensation, of smell and touch and not one where a child makes sharp and informed distinctions between people, events and causality as I had depicted it earlier. Thus, this dreamy, sensuous and non-intellectual world of children, coupled with indirection, where the damage has already been done, so to speak, was to become a hallmark of my technique in writing about violence associated with the war. The result: less physical acts of violence.

"The Bhudis" opens with the child narrator's aunt having been beaten to near-death already, lying on a bed, in a hut full of guerillas, one of whom, Squinty, wants to instill further pain on the woman. The actual beating of the narrator's aunt is mentioned in passing: "They beat her with sticks as big as the one Grandpa used to kill a thick snake in the fields one day. They beat her until she couldn't move or cry. They just thrashed her like *rapoko*"[1] (7). The rest of the story is a dramatization of the hostilities between the two guerilla groups in the hut. The reader soon realizes that the commanders of both groups are selfishly fighting over the possession of the woman's body for sex. The tension in "The Bhudis" is heightened by a parallel incident – the impending death through burning, of the child narrator's grandmother. The grandmother has been falsely accused of witchcraft by one of the neighbours. The story ends as the child hopelessly tries to rescue his grandmother. Finally, I could feel the story and it took me back to that day in 1978, when I was six, the day the bhudis nearly beat my aunt to death. With hindsight, "The Bhudis" has several marks of apprenticeship but I was rewarded with what I thought was a princely sum, then, of $500 by Modus Publications. I could write after all. Write about war.

Indirection is at work as well in "Heads and Tails" (2005). Three boys enjoy pinning lizards to the ground and watching them shed their tails. If the lizard does not shed its tail, the boys chop off the tail with their small axes. They are thrilled by the lashing of the tails. An argument ensues about what happens to both the body and head of a beheaded person. The question is directed at Jafethi, whose father has recently been arrested for avenging the death of his mother during the war. Jafethi's father, a guerilla just come back from the war, beheads Simoni, the man who had accused Jafethi's grandmother of witchcraft, resulting in her death. The story actually happened in our village. Instead of foregrounding the beheading, my story focuses on the taunting of the man's son by two boys who want Jafethi to explain what happens to a beheaded body. Lameck, one of the two malicious boys, asks Jafethi, "Didn't he [Jafethi's father] tell you what it's like, Jafethi? Besides, my mother says he did it because he over-did it during the war. She says it's a curse. His brain is boiling from the innocent blood he shed" (35). There is a sense of inherited outrage over this murder, the slaughter of a human being "like a goat" (35) but it is misdirected. The narrator attempts to defend both Jafethi and his father's actions but he is out of his depth and ends up invoking God. Even that is not enough as the omniscience and omnipotence of God are both questioned by the two slightly grown-up children, Lameck and Mbonisi. The latter asks, "Do you mean to tell me that he can see the smallest of ants?" (36). More questions follow. Does God know how many ants there are in the world? Does he know about the pain of each and every ant? How about the pain of the lizard's tail? Does he know how many mosquitoes there are in the world?

To clear his confusion, the narrator in "Heads and Tails" looks for an answer about hell from his mother who gives him the biblical version of a vast lake of fire. When he asks his grandfather, the old man studies the boy's palms and says, "Hell was the war. There's still another hell I hope you won't fall into. As far as your hands show, not too bad. That hell, my grandson, is poverty" (38). In other words, although the story is based on murder and revenge, it focuses on the children's understanding of issues around this, suggesting more questions than answers.

The horror that the child narrator witnesses in "The Boy With A Crooked Head" (2006), decomposing corpses being eaten by dogs, is too ghastly to render coherently. As a result, the narrative is fractured and the narrator is unreliable. The child narrator was actually inspired by my cousin who resulted from the rape of my aunt by the guerillas in "The Bhudis." It was a family secret that ended up as common knowledge when several rituals were performed to "settle" my cousin. He was generally violent to other children, played truant at school and was incredibly forgetful. In the story, the narrator declares:

> I don't understand much. I told you. Ask Uncle Finias who says my father might have died in the first war of guns against white people. Nobody knows him, not even my mother. That's why my head is not straight. A boy whose father is not known cannot have a straight head.

Perhaps my father too, like Uncle Vikitha, disappeared into the smoke of a war (6).

I thought that a character like this one could best report the utmost horror because the reader may not initially trust the narrator but eventually do as the narrative progresses and therein the effectiveness lay. This is not to say I worked it out as neatly as that. If anything, I was scared of my memories around this story. Casting the narrator as my cousin was a way of vicariously dealing with the horror.

The poignancy of the story relies on the parallel between the pariah status of the "useless" narrator and his "useless" Uncle Vikitha. The uncle, "a useless person who spends his time chasing after old women" and "gets very drunk and sings at the top of his voice all kinds of obscenities" (3), according to the boy's grandmother, disappears soon after the departure of "Soldiers with radios that went sh…sh….sh… most of the time" (1). Uncle Vikitha is based on my uncle who was killed during the Gukurahundi. The delayed graphic detail of the horror, the climax, occurs just before the end of the story. The raw material comes from my Entumbane experience. My father had gone to our rural home, leaving me alone in our Entumbane house when the second battle of 1981 erupted. I was lucky to flee Entumbane. Three days later, I came back. The shops were closed. I couldn't buy any food. But we had a little field of ripe corn just outside our house. I went into the field of tall, dense green maize plants. The following description is largely that of the two dead soldiers I saw amongst the maize plants. I write in "The Boy With A Crooked Head," and I think I should quote at length here:

> It was the smell. It shot through my nostrils, sat in my head and refused to leave.
>
> It's still in my head. From my head it dived into my stomach and scooped out all the sadza and milk I had this morning before setting off to herd cattle. Then there was something like the growling of dogs and droning of bees behind a thicket from which the smell was coming.
>
> Two dogs were snarling at each other, their mouths quivering. In between them was the leg of a person from which clouds of flies buzzed away when the dogs moved nearer and buzzed back when the dogs moved away. One dog was licking the shiny dome of a skull with punctured eyes as if both eyes were slyly winking.
>
> Then I saw two other skulls and what looked like a heap of green-blue *mathumbu* [intestines]. I left the rest of the milk and sadza on the ground

and my stomach continued heaving and heaving. Drunk with the smell, I ran, stumbling.

Because I knew if I didn't run, the smell would choke me to death. I ran. And ran (5).

At this stage of my writing, I had learnt that real life incidents could migrate and merge freely depending on the desired effect. I also learnt something – the importance of smell. The sense of smell has become such an integral part of my writing.

"Stampede" (2008) focalises a soldier who has done a lot of killing himself. It is an attempt to understand the reasons a soldier kills. It was a difficult story to write. This story is bare of details and relies on an even more unreliable narrator battling forgetfulness. Jekoniya, the soldier in the story, is in a "never ending war in peace time" (134). The situation is a surreal one. Jekoniya hears the voice of the Great Leader "troubling the roof of the winter sky." He vaguely feels the rest of his brigade "around somewhere... but [does] not see them" (134). He does not know how he came to resign himself to a zombie-like existence. The only part that refers explicitly to Jekoniya's exploits is very brief and matter-of-fact:

> There were so many things that Jekoniya couldn't remember. Very strange because a few weeks or months ago, he had been firing at some enemies in a war in another country not his own nor the Great Leader's. Did those enemies fire back? Or did he just pick them off like sitting ducks? At times it happened that way. Orders (134).

The idea is not to judge Jekoniya. He is infantilised, so to speak, made unreliable, so that the reader engages with Jekoniya without judiciously criticising him. As in the child's point of view, the reader is being asked to supply ethical distinctions for him/herself.

As the story progresses, Jekoniya hears the Great Leader's order to get ready and fight but notices he has a rusty AK 47 instead of the three weapons, two of which he remembers leaving in his mother's hut – a grenade "the size of the Great Leader's fist" (134) and a bazooka. He walks home to fetch the two weapons. He walks for three days and nights through "Leafless trees [that] stretched as far as Jekoniya's eyes could see – a nest of twisted limbs and gnarled fingers like a giant fish net" (135). When he arrives home, he is confronted by the absence of life, and ruins:

> ... there was no smoke coiling out of the gap between the wall and thatch. There were no chickens scratching the ground for food. There was no smell of cow dung from the cattle pen. No mooing, no tinkling of

bells. The kitchen door had fallen into the hut and termites were feasting on it. Yes, the sturdy *umvagazi*[2] door had been reduced to paper thinness. (136).

Jekoniya's relatives are gone. Even in this story, people disappear or leave:

> He hoped for the smell of smoke-cured thatch but it didn't come, no matter how hard he sniffed the air. He sniffed the air until he became dizzy. Then it came, from inside him – the smell of several departures. Everybody had left. His mother, his two brothers and younger sister, Khethiwe. Where had they all gone? Ah, when he looked through the hole in the roof he saw footprints... cutting through the bush, disappearing into the Limpopo River... (136).

But this time it is hunger that makes people leave.

At this point, those familiar with the political situation in Zimbabwe will notice that this is an allusion to the way Robert Mugabe, through the military, has held the country at ransom and in the process caused untold suffering. The excesses of the Mugabe regime have destroyed families through mass emigration. Accelerated death through HIV/AIDS because of the absence of drugs and food is a serious form of aggression. Thousands flee the invisible war of thwarted dreams and hunger caused by a botched land reform. I write in the story:

> There was nothing in the hut, not even a piece of broken pottery. Tufts of dry grass stuck out of the floor at the back of the hut. Maybe his [Jekoniya's] mother was buried in that very same hut and her emaciated remains had nourished the grass in summer. Buried with her pots and her broken pieces of pottery, killed by hunger.
>
> The last time he had been home he had brought a lot of food. The Great Leader had given them food in the army. His mother had been on the brink of dying from starvation and found it difficult to swallow anything. They had forced her to drink watery porridge. When was he last here? (136)

The absence of war, as some people correctly assert, does not mean peace. On top of failing to recover his weapons, Jekoniya also discovers that the big house that had stood in front of the hut, the house whose building he financed, has disappeared. He thinks the big grenade must have blown it up, "Blown up everything into thin air. Blown up his education too. His mother had insisted that his certificate be gilt-framed and hung in the living room..." (137). Even education becomes meaningless. The absence of his family and the big house reminds Jekoniya of "a secret sorrow, secret even from himself." He suspects it could be "the sorrow of hunger" since hunger had made him join the army. But that is not it, for "There was a greater sorrow. Something he had lost. Something buried in infinite folds of frustration and many years of shooting at many enemies.... Was his sorrow forgetfulness?" (138). Jekoniya, in my assessment, has forgotten what it is to be human.

When Jekoniya rejoins his brigade, the commander tells him of a plan to abandon The Great Leader, not take his orders to fight. Jekoniya cannot see the faces of his fellow soldiers but just the "outlines of their faces" (139). They are faceless and the commander speaks through an "absent mouth" (139). The Great Leader announces that his loyal soldiers are coming after deserters and that sparks a stampede. The stampede is a recollection and re-working of running blindly in the hail of bullets in the second Entumbane clash. Jekoniya keeps on running until, in the end, tired and getting stampeded, he laughs bitterly when it dawns on him that probably everyone has fled the Great Leader.

The use of parallel incidents to create the right mood and atmosphere is also something that I learnt in writing about war or violence. This prepares the reader for the shocking violence or aftermath of such violence. It also foreshadows some of the action.

In "The Bhudis", the grandmother's cat sustains broken ribs and dies because it is suspected that she rides the cat at night on her witching rounds. In "Heads and Tails" the boys chop off lizards' tails. Cattle spoil for a fight in "The Boy With A Crooked Head." They do so on the spot where Ntombi, a cow that the boy liked so much, was killed. Someone had broken the cow's leg and axed her several times on the neck and backside. The boy recalls the end of Ntombi:

> So when Ntombi wobbled into the kraal yesterday with flies humming like an aeroplane high up in the sky and maggots wriggling like a bunch of crazy white wires in her sores, Uncle Finias, the one who has not disappeared, said, "Let's finish her off." With a huge sweep, the large sharp axe glinted briefly in the sun before sinking into Ntombi's neck, just behind her head. She trembled and mooed in a tired way, tongue lolling out. The axe shone again in the sun, with some blood on it and fell again. I didn't wait for the rest. I didn't eat Ntombi's meat (1-2).

This foreshadows the boy's discovery of rotting corpses behind a thicket. The isolation of the child coupled with these incidents emphasises the unrelenting grip of violence and abandonment.

It was difficult to construct or reconstruct the language, tone and diction of a young person – especially given that I wanted to use that perspective to write about war. Writing the stories discussed here made me realise that the child's point of view is more contrived than any other and more susceptible to sentimentality and artificiality than, perhaps, any other. One strategy of avoiding a gush of sentimentality in the three stories I wrote from a child's view was to give children agency. In "The Bhudis," the child is inquisitive and attacks the "evil Squinty," innocuously, of course, but the fighting spirit is there. In "Heads and Tails" children are not involved in innocent frolics but perpetrate their own brand of violence. They inflict psychological pain on one of their playmates. In "The Boy With A Crooked Head," the narrator is not blameless either as he finds beating up the children who torment him enjoyable and therapeutic.

It's been a journey. Thinking about events I would rather not think about and writing about them. These days, Mother and I talk a lot. Not about the war, but other things. My late grandfather was a palmist and he is the old man who reads the boy's palms in "Heads and Tails." My dear departed grandfather, I think you were wrong. Mugabe has made me and a lot of others very poor. He quietly fights us every day. Mother says my only child, my ten year old son, needs a playmate. Should she talk to my wife? I say no. Why don't we have another child? I tell her living in Zimbabwe, with a collapsed economy and all the things that make life almost impossible, is like living in a war zone. Who wants to bring a life into a war that doesn't look like it will end soon? She says children were being born during the war. Have I forgotten that my late sister was born during the war? Besides, she adds, terrible things can happen. If this one child is taken away from me (meaning if he dies), what am I going to do? I should talk to my wife about this. What are we going to do if our son is taken away from us?

References

Ndlovu, T. (1993), "The Bhudis." *Sunday Gazette Magazine*, 18 July 1993 (p.7).

___(2005), "Heads and Tails." In J. Kangira (Ed.), *Creatures Great and Small* (pp34-39). Gweru: Mambo Press.

___(2006), 'The Boy With A Crooked Head." In J. Morris (Ed.), Short Writings from Bulawayo III (pp 1-6).

___(2008), "Stampede." In Morris, J. (Ed.), *Long Time Coming: Short Writings from Zimbabwe* (pp134-140).

Notes

[1] Finger millet.

[2] A hard wood. The name literally means "the tree that bleeds" because of its red sap.

Chapter 8

SEASONS OF TRAGEDY AND HOPE

Michael Woodman

My forehead rests against the window. The shrill vibration reminds me uncomfortably that we are hovering three thousand feet above the desert. The ground below is almost featureless. Drab brown terrain arches towards the horizon, occasionally split by a snaking dry riverbed or a remote human settlement, small clusters of round tukuls with fine webs of paths fanning into the desert. I can just make out the long shadows of donkeys drinking at waterholes gouged into the dry riverbeds. I notice black rings tattooed onto the desert floor where fires have consumed tukuls.

"Janjaweed," Ibrahim shouts to me above the din of the rotor blades noting my gaze.

"Devil on horseback," he translates.

The ungainly Russian helicopter sinks slowly through the hot air. As it banks, I see a massive rock towering proud from the desert. Ibrahim tells me that it almost completely encircles a valley forming a natural fortress which is the stronghold of the main rebel movement fighting for autonomy for Darfur from the government.

The pilot doesn't shut down the engine, so I jog, crouched, towards the waiting vehicle to escape the drooping blades whooshing overhead and the blast of heat and dust from the exhaust.

We drive directly to the small town, nothing more than a village of makeshift thatched tukuls, a small bazaar and a clinic. It is home to around three thousand local inhabitants who are now hosting at least fourteen thousand Darfurians displaced from their own villages by attacks by Janjaweed militiamen. Some of the more established tukuls are surrounded by thickets of thorn bushes – designed to keep donkeys and sheep within the compound at night. We are directed to a community leader.

"Salaam aleikum!" he greets us warmly, despite his apparent surprise.

"Wa aleikum salaam!" Ibrahim returns the peace greeting and proceeds to translate the man's lament.

"Many children have died in the last few weeks from diarrhoea and fever. There are no medicines and no doctors here. The food is finished. Our store from last harvest was burnt in the fires and we fled with just the clothes on our backs. It is still some time before the planting season. If people get very ill, they have to risk the five-hour journey south to the nearest hospital but convoys are often attacked and robbed on the way. Most often we just stay here and pray to Allah, the Merciful and Compassionate. In the end it is His will."

He takes us to a barren area on the edge of the settlement. There I count fourteen fresh unmarked dark mounds studding the sand of the cemetery.

"Are there other children who are sick now?" I ask through Ibrahim.

He ponders for a moment, and then says, "Yes."

He then leads us down the sandy track to a compound where he calls out to a young woman. She takes us to a shaded wooden platform at the edge of the compound. I notice a deep scar and indentation across her forehead. An emaciated child lies gasping on her side with diarrhoea oozing from her fleshless body. Flaky skin is draped over her skeleton and flies buzz around her like vultures circling over a dying animal. We explain to the young mother that we would like to take her child to the clinic to commence treatment. She appears resigned to the fate of her child and is busy breastfeeding her youngest child. Eventually she agrees after a hushed conversation with her husband, a handsome, imposing figure with a thick, black beard. He is obviously much older than she.

We take Zachia and her mother to the clinic and start treatment. The ward is a single open room in which there are four string beds. There is neither electricity nor water.

I see her the next morning. Her bony frame lies limp under the mosquito net; her big saucer-like eyes are brown pools of apathy. Her chest heaves to draw air into her lungs and she is becoming increasingly exhausted. It is too late and, like her mother, I too resign myself to the fact that she will die.

On the fourth day she is miraculously still clinging to life. I look into her wide staring eyes and wonder if she registers anything. I start to see subtle signs of improvement: the fever is coming down, her breathing slightly easier and the diarrhoea is slowing. She is still far from safe, but over the next week she improves gradually. She is sipping the specially formulated milk feeds and the hollows of her cheeks are starting to fill. There is renewed hope in her young mother who now caresses her, smiles and sings soothing lullabies in the local language. I ask her mother how she got the scar on her forehead but she shakes her head, clicks her tongue and doesn't want to talk. A nurse tells me that her husband is known to beat her. Zachia continues to improve and after three weeks is ready to go home.

I meet Asha at the clinic for the first time. She is thirteen years old, high cheek-boned with doe eyes and intricately plaited hair pulled tightly back from her high forehead. She is painfully shy and finds it difficult to make eye contact. I want to hear her story and not her mother's version. She presents a crumpled card with some scribbles of an old prescription for monthly antibiotic injections dated before the conflict started. I examine her. The whooshing heart murmur and swelling of her ankles indicate that she has mild heart failure, probably caused by a bout of rheumatic fever as a child as a result of an untreated skin infection. I start her on the appropriate medication and ask her to come back in a week. Over the next months I see Asha regularly. The medication appears to be working well. Her new clinic treatment card is neatly folded in a transparent plastic cover that she keeps tied inside a second black plastic bag for extra protection. She doesn't know what the scribbles on the card mean but she guards it as a prized possession. She starts to smile; she makes eye contact and tells me she is feeling much stronger and is joining the other girls preparing the fields for the planting season. Each day they plough furrows into the earth with hand-held hoes. Later she tells me excitedly that they are now sowing seeds as the rains are approaching.

Dark clouds pregnant with rain gather on the horizon. The heat and the dust build and finally white bolts of lightning streak to earth unleashing booming thunder and torrents of rain. The desert thirstily blots up the lashing rain. The rain falls and falls and the rivers now gush with muddy water rippling over the sandy bed; eating into the banks. Large islands of sand collapse into the flow. The sodden earth delivers tiny green shoots that take root, flourish and push upwards.

I take great pleasure in seeing Asha doing so well. Like the crops in the earth, she is blooming into womanhood, full of hopes and dreams for the life ahead of her.

BOOM, BOOM, BOOM, BOOM; gunfire shatters the stillness of the night.

I roll onto the floor instinctively, staring upwards in the direction of the bullets hissing above the thatch roof. My heart pounds with raw fear and I try to reassure myself that any bullet would have to pass through two mud brick walls to reach me. I assume the heavy calibre fire is spewing from the truck-mounted anti-aircraft gun at the nearby military camp. It intensifies and is now answered by the crackle of smaller calibre fire spattering from one direction then another. An engine screams and revs in low gear. Footsteps; urgent shouting; then voices are outside my hut. The door swings open but from the floor I can't identify the robed silhouette.

"I am Mohammed," comes the familiar but breathless voice of our guard. "Man shoot, come!"

I dress hurriedly. A wounded man is being carried into the compound followed by a crowd of men and a few women. I direct them to the tent and ask for the generator to be started.

The man is in agony. He hangs around the necks of two men who are supporting his legs. His white trousers are ripped and wrapped tightly and knotted around his right knee as an improvised bandage which is dark and glistening. His name is Farid and he is the younger brother of the local chief. He is laid on the table in the makeshift operating theatre, a canvas tent. I open the bandage. Several bullets have ripped through the knee leaving shards of gleaming bone amidst a mangle of flesh. I quickly cover the wound and lean hard down on it to stem the bleeding. The midwife sets up the drip and injects the general anaesthetic whilst I finish donning a surgical gown and scrubbing my hands. I start to work, stopping occasionally to swipe in vain at the gathering swarm of flies.

We finally leave the operating tent as dawn breaks and I strip out of the bloodied surgical gown. Farid is waking but woozy under the cocktail of anaesthetic and painkiller. He will not lose his leg but will never walk normally again.

Sleep won't come; my eyes dart restlessly in the darkness behind my closed lids. Eventually I drift into a fitful sleep punctuated by vivid dreams: I am kidnapped by rebels at gunpoint, taken by horse to their cave and operate on their wounded colleagues in a cave by candlelight.

The atmosphere in the town is becoming increasingly tense. A food convoy has been attacked and several people killed. We balance the need to stay to serve the population against the increasing threat to our personal safety. After agonising discussions we unanimously decide to evacuate to the town further south which is relatively stable. I feel guilt as we drive through the town towards the helicopter landing area; solemn eyes follow our journey registering our departure. We are the lucky ones who are able to leave.

We arrive in the town and I am physically and mentally numb. Fever is coming and going, breaking in sweats and shivers. I lie outstretched on the bed and stare up at the ceiling fan creaking rhythmically and sending a soothing down-draft of air.

I go to a dilapidated clinic near the bazaar and sit on the laboratory bench watching the technician squinting studiously down the antique microscope.

"No malaria!" he looks up at me confidently.

"You sure?" I ask, unable to hide my disappointment, as I still don't know why I am ill. I decide not to treat myself and thankfully improve over the next two days.

The news spreads that there is heavy fighting in the north. I speak via radio with Ibrahim who has the keys to the pharmacy and he takes dressings and drugs to the clinic so that the wounded can be treated. A week later the situation has calmed significantly. We decide to go back and spend the day scouring the bazaar for luxury groceries, mainly oranges and mangoes – the favourite to break the monotonous diet of beans and bread.

We arrive at mid morning and go directly to the clinic where there is a figure lying on a narrow wooden bench. Her face is so swollen that the features are unrecognisable. Her clinic record is in a neat plastic cover resting across her stomach. I pick it up and my fear is confirmed; it is Asha. Her whole body is bloated and when I push her ankles, my fingers leave deep pits sunk in her skin. Her condition has deteriorated and her heart is failing to pump, effectively leaving fluid building up in her tissues. Her family has brought her to the clinic as soon as they heard of our arrival. I start treatment with a diuretic to try and shift the fluid and ease her failing heart. There is no response. I inject all of the vials left in our stock praying that there will be some result.

There is nothing more we can do, so we discuss the option of sending her on the five-hour truck journey to the main town. It is the last remaining hope. Her parents weigh up the risks and agree, desperate to give her every chance to survive. We are lucky that there is a convoy leaving that afternoon. We negotiate with the driver who asks for extra pay to carry her in the cabin protected from the sun and dust. Her uncle volunteers to travel with her. Before she leaves, I shake her shoulder gently. "Asha, Asha, Asha!"

She just looks at me. It is difficult to read any expression, but there is no fear in her eyes, only disappointment.

The military is increasingly present in the area and is trying to secure control of a village near the mountain. A military convoy arrives at the clinic in an impressive fleet of trucks mounted with anti-aircraft weapons.

I ask them politely to leave the compound. The young soldiers swagger and wave their weapons at me. I find the commanding officer who understands my request and orders his men off the compound. The civilians waiting at the clinic breathe a silent sigh of relief.

Later that day, the military are back. A soldier has fallen from a high truck injuring his leg and back. He is disorientated and aggressive and is carried to the tent. They say he does not drink any alcohol but mumble about maybe having smoked something. He is thrashing around on the examination bed and I am unable to assess him. He swears and spits at me and suddenly I feel my temper surge within me to exploding point. The midwife who is assisting me senses my anger and casts me a sharp reproaching look and I control myself. Eventually, he settles after an injection of pain killer and we are able to plaster his broken leg. I am also worried that he may have injured his spine. We have no X-ray facility, so we admit him to the ward whilst the military radio for a vehicle or helicopter to evacuate him to the nearest hospital.

A man walks into the clinic followed by a stooped veiled woman. I recognise him as Asha's uncle. The woman sweeps back the veil revealing the anguished face of Asha's mother. She is red-eyed from tears and sleepless nights. She hands me Asha's clinic card and I read that the doctors tried to treat her but it was too late. She died the day after arriving at the hospital. Her uncle had to arrange a quick burial in that foreign town with no way of informing her parents. I picture him lowering Asha into the sandy earth with the help of a grave-digger, laying her on her right side facing Mecca.

Her mother is now sobbing openly and says she misses her so much. I hand her back the clinic card and she puts it back in the plastic cover, clutching it like a prized possession. My eyes sting and start to water.

At mid morning, there is a buzz of murmuring at the clinic. News is spreading that three girls have been kidnapped by the Janjaweed whilst collecting firewood several kilometres from the town. A search party of young men on horseback are gathering. They are dressed in greens and browns with turbans wrapped around their heads and Kalashnikovs strung over their shoulders glinting in the morning sun. The horses are wild-eyed and agitated sensing their owners' intoxicating blend of fear and excitement. The search party returns without the girls late the following night. They have had exchanges of fire with the captors, but have not been able to free the girls. One young man has been killed on the spot and another has taken a bullet in his thigh. His comrades have led his horse through the night to our compound. He is tired and weak from loss of blood and slides heavily off his mount.

I operate on him in the early hours of the morning.

His friends chatter outside the tent; young men buzzing with adrenaline, lack of sleep and the bond of having been in battle together. I plan to admit him to the ward. He will need several days of antibiotics and a second operation to close the open wound.

The soldier with the broken leg is still in the ward. I agonise over what to do as it may create serious problems placing a rebel and an army soldier in the same room but there are no other options. Both men are in unquestionable need of medical treatment.

I stick to the principle that we are impartial and neutral. Every individual is equal in our eyes whether a government soldier or a 'rebel', and I am reminded again of that overused cliché that one man's 'rebel' is another's 'freedom fighter'. So I admit the 'rebel' to the ward and there are now two in-patients. There is a lot of murmuring and I sense the distrust and hatred but neither man is in a position to leave. The tension gradually eases. By the second day, there is some jovial banter between the visitors of both patients. The soldier's colleagues seem to have more means and bring him sweets every day that they have bought in the bazaar. The next day a military ambulance is available to transfer the soldier to the main town. I write the discharge papers. As he is being carried out of the ward on a stretcher, he asks to stop at the bed of the rebel. They exchange words in Arabic; hands reach out and meet in a clasp and then the soldier hands over his remaining bags of sweets which the rebel accepts with a nod of acknowledgment.

A man arrives at the gate leading a horse and asks if I would be willing to help. He explains that it is one of the horses from the search party the previous night. The mare has a bullet hole in the left side of her chest which is sucking air in with each shallow breath she takes. I patch the hole. He puts his hands together and gives a short bow of thanks before leading the mare to his compound not far from our own. Two days later, vultures are circling above.

"It is God's will," he tells me as I walk past.

The three missing girls walk back into town. We are very eager to speak to them to find out if they have been assaulted in any way, but it is a very sensitive issue. If they are known to have been raped, it will bring untold shame on themselves and their families and could seriously affect chances of marriage. Fatima, the nurse, manages to make contact with them and they agree to meet her in secret. They all deny any rape and I am relieved when Fatima says she believes them. They have, however, been beaten with sticks and there are thin red welts on their backs and legs. They say their captors wanted to know how many men, guns and vehicles are in the town.

The sun sinks low and the fields are a rich green in the dusk light. The crops are now tall and it is nearing harvesting time. I follow the sandy path meandering through the wheat towards the small town. I see a crowd gathered at the clinic compound and I can make out Abakar, the medical assistant. He is not in his usual working clothes but strikes a regal figure in a crisp white flowing gown, white skull cap and is leaning on a brass cane.

He is talking with Hawagul, the midwife. A wooden donkey cart is parked against the clinic building.

"Very bad," Abakar shakes his head from side to side as I come into earshot.

This is not 'men's business' but Hawagul explains to the family that it is important for me to see the woman and ushers me in. Hawagul has erected a sheet around the bed to provide some semblance of privacy. She speaks to the woman hurriedly in local language, hands me a pair of gloves and flicks on her torch. I follow the beam to the young woman on the bed. Her face is exhausted and etched with the grimace of constant pain. She went into labour the day before whilst working in the fields near the Chadian frontier but the baby wouldn't come. She parts her legs and my shoulders slump with what I see: the swollen blue hand and forearm of a baby protrudes from her. Her womb contracts and she raises her head straining against her clenched teeth. The arm descends slightly but retracts as she slumps back after the contraction.

I listen for the baby's heart, pressing the cone against her abdomen and praying to hear the familiar 'tap' 'tap' 'tap' 'tap' of a baby's heart. Nothing. I try again, this time my eyes screwed tightly shut, willing my hearing to be my only sense. Silence. The baby is dead. The baby's shoulder is stuck at the outlet of the womb; the neck bent and the head still well within the womb. We try to manipulate the baby but it is hopeless. I am very worried; she is exhausted and her womb hard with the pushing against an impossible task. I take the difficult decision to operate. Her womb may rupture and she may die if I don't. If I do, she may die from a complication of the anaesthetic or operation under these extreme conditions. We discuss it with her and her husband. He helps her to make a mark on the consent form to undergo a caesarean section before signing himself. Her relatives carry her on a stretcher to the operating tent. We prepare the 'theatre' and equipment. I have sent a guard to call Abakar from home to inject the anaesthetic. I read my textbook as it has been seven years since I last performed this operation alone. I silently perform the procedure in my mind's eye: incision, retraction, incision, deliver baby, clamps, sutures, knot, sutures, knot, close. There is no margin for error. We decide to try one more time to deliver the baby in the hope of avoiding an operation. Somehow we manoeuvre the dead baby into a position where it delivers. The ordeal is over and the woman lies back exhausted but she is alive, and for that I am deeply relieved.

The hot dry harmattan winds are whipping the desert sands into flight. Dark clouds of sand billow across the plains, driving sand into every crevice and leaving the gritty taste of earth in the mouth. A donkey-drawn cart emerges from the sand storm sweeping from the east. A blanket covers a body on the back of the cart providing a protective cocoon from the stinging sand.

A young man beckons me over and draws back the top of the blanket. Squinting up at me is an old woman. Her pale face bears the wrinkles of the passage of many seasons and is pale. Her name is Fatima and she is the mother of eight children, four still living.

No one can tell me how old she is. She doesn't know and someone volunteers 'eighty,' but there is a lot of disagreement. I write 'sixty' on the treatment card.

She tells me she has never been to a clinic or hospital before and is very scared. She says she thinks she will die. I tell her not to worry, although I am not sure. She is carried to the tent and I examine her. Her loose papery skin is hot to touch.

Finally, I find the cause of her illness. She has a vesico-vaginal fistula, an internal connection between vagina and rectum, usually a result of prolonged childbirth and no access to medical care. The other cause is rape.

I ask for a volunteer to donate blood as she desperately needs a transfusion. All of her male relatives volunteer immediately, which surprises me as I have noted that men are often reluctant to donate. She is the matriarch.

We sit in the tent chatting with the men ranging from young to old as we test each sample. We find a match from her young nephew and take a pint of blood from him which we transfuse directly into her. She looks bewildered at the tube feeding blood into her vein as if the arm does not belong to her. The transfusion and antibiotics start to take effect and she picks up over the next few days. By the end of the week, she is sitting and eating. The following week, she starts shuffling unsteadily. She is too old and unfit for an operation to repair her problem and is not willing to travel as it is too unsafe. She wants to go home.

She is freshly bathed and dressed and sitting on the clinic step waiting for her son to fetch her. I sit silently beside her and the afternoon sun bathes our faces as we watch the cart approaching from the east.

The time is coming for me to leave. I take a last walk towards the bazaar. A man approaching me on the path stops me and takes my hand. He rummages in his sack and pulls out a small rectangular leather parchment. Inside it he places a neatly folded piece of paper with Arabic symbols written on it and seals it.

"Qu'ran," he says.

He ties it around my neck and, with a smile, continues on his way.

Ibrahim explains later that it is a local charm for protection against evils including bullets and it is highly effective. But I say I have seen many young men wearing this 'protection' who have been shot. He chuckles and shrugs.

I continue and come across a food aid distribution. The only shade is cast by a gnarled tree under which stand a mosaic of colourfully dressed women. The men are nearby in a line being called forward to receive large sacks of grain marked with the flags of some far off wealthy country.

As I walk past, I hear my name being called. A young woman approaches me, one arm around an infant saddled against her hip. I recognise her as Zachia's mother with the distinctive deep furrow across her forehead. She is beaming and pointing at her child. "Zachia! Zachia, Zachia!"

I recognise her by her stern expression and eyes. Her face has filled out and her cheeks border on chubby.

"Zachia!" I reach out to shake her hand. She takes my hand gingerly with her little fingers. Her big dark eyes smile at me.

Postscript

It is nearly a year since the passage of these seasons in Darfur and still there is no resolution in sight. I now find myself back working in my home country, Zimbabwe, in which a different kind of catastrophe is unfolding. I witness tragedies daily.

But it is the smallest acts of kindness and compassion that kindle the flicker of hope.

I dedicate this piece to the memory of Asha and the countless others who will never realise their hopes and dreams as a result of an armed conflict.

Chapter 9

AFRICA'S WORLD WAR: A CONGOLESE JOURNEY

Kevin Eze

The plane made the steep, tactical descent to the N'djili International Airport. It was a pleasant flight if you put aside the delay in Douala. As soon as the aircraft stopped, I grabbed my luggage and headed for the arrival lounge. I slung off my hand luggage, pulled out my documents, and joined the queue that wove erratically through the sizzling lounge behind the counter marked *'étrangers'* – for 'foreigners'.

Security was tight and the lounge was flooded with officers and civilians who roamed strangely around. Each check lasted several minutes. If you let go of your luggage, it will be taken. If you get distracted, you will be robbed. If you converse or if you let something grab your attention, someone will pick your pocket. Then came my turn to check in. The officer behind the counter was drinking Coca-Cola and smoking Marlboros. I turned in my passport. He looked at it, mumbled a few words, and directed me to another officer to his left. The officer was named Boyoma – a no-neck linebacker with teeth like corn kernels and hands like T-bone steaks. He looked bizarrely at my Nigerian passport, raised his left eyebrow that was separated by a gummy black scar, and asked me to pay a hundred dollars or something if I wished to enter the country. He added that he was being kind. He only wanted to hurt those who hurt the Congolese. If he went down, he would go down as did Patrice Lumumba.

I was in Kinshasa, the Democratic Republic of the Congo, a high emerald country in the foothills of the Congo River. The Democratic Republic of the Congo was destined to become an African super giant. It had all the makings of an uplifting narrative. Two-thirds the size of Western Europe, but ten times less populated. The land beneath the country that used to be known as Zaïre is fantastically rich. The country enjoys an enviable geographical situation at the crossroads of West, Central, East and southern Africa.

At the time of independence, our fathers – Boyoma's and mine – had hoped that Zaïre would form the Francophone pillar of Nigeria and South Africa, a pillar of stability and development that would extend to the whole of sub-Saharan Africa. But as I entered the DR Congo, nothing distinguished it from a crisis-torn nation.

I crossed the checkpoint. In the whirlpool of touts and thieves, I saw a man holding a placard marked with my name. He introduced himself as Kasavuvu, a faculty staff. He led me to a beaten up 4x4 Toyota pickup and we drove off to the Jesuit College. The Jesuit College, a collection of one-storey fancy-block buildings interrupted by verandas and bright green lawns, stood on a sixty-acre base in the hills just outside of the capital Kinshasa. As I brought down my luggage from the vehicle, I heard the mooing of cows, the bleating of sheep and the war song of the 7th Battalion, 34th Squadron.

I was like the other students from various countries of Africa. All of us, just about, had been admitted as students of Humanities and Philosophy. For three years or more, we would stuff our minds with the best and worst of human thoughts. Kasavuvu wished me *bonne chance*, and the gates of the Jesuit College drew closed behind me.

I walked up to the notice board, looked at the list of freshmen and found my name next to Mukasa Hostel. I followed the direction upstairs. The stairs creaked and groaned and made the kind of noises that old school stairs make when students have gone up and down them for ages. I had no problem with that as long as they didn't collapse under me. With time I'd know which step squeaked and which one peeped and where to tread if I wanted to walk unnoticed.

Upstairs, all the florescent lamps were on and all the doors stood open. I entered the door that bore my name and put down my luggage. The room was warm and neat. I came out almost immediately, closed the door and strolled along the wide and desolate veranda overlooking a huge rain forest. I went to the furthest end and caught an aerial view of Kinshasa at night. I said nothing. Drained from the long trip from Lagos to Douala, and after several hours of lay over to Kinshasa, I returned to my room at a snail's pace, took a shower, and got ready to sleep. The bed was as narrow and constricted as the squeaky stairs. I enjoyed a quiet night.

Not for long. I woke up to the cracking sounds of military helicopters roving the sky above the college's roof. Quietly, I climbed onto a chair and peered at a myriad of green helicopters. The roofs looked broader and more timid and the horizon seemed diminished. I looked at everything around me and knew that soon I would be done for. The helicopters moved further away as if encircling the palm-studded forest from where vociferous sporadic shootings ensued. The floor of my room shook as if I would sink into the earth. No din and no clamor – just shooting and shooting and shooting.

Before long, scores of sergeants emerged from the bush, their faces darkened from the scorching sun, their biceps trembling from fatigue, their palms smelling of rifle smear.

They rushed into the college's refectory scrambling for something to eat and drink. They were government forces, a jumble of troops from Angola, Namibia and Zimbabwe. They talked about AFDL and UNITA and FDLR and MONUC. They did push-ups in the lawn and referred to seven o'clock as "nineteen hundred hours." They would high-five and shout, "Maudit soit l'ennemi" – or "Cursed be the enemy." Some had blood splattered on their foreheads and the blood streaked down their temples from their hair. After a few hours, all the soldiers activated, climbed onto a grey military van, pressed their arms to their bloodthirsty rifles and gave the Jesuit College the bravest, most confident smiles you can imagine. They shipped off for N'djili Airport. Soon I heard prolonged sounds of random shootings coming from the direction of the airport.

On the TV, I saw that several thousands had been killed and several thousand houses burnt down. The rebels carried out their gruesome task with a variety of weapons – AK-47 assault rifles, grenades, and pangas (the all-purpose, heavy-bladed machetes). I felt like vomiting. I turned off the TV and tiptoed to the gate as I'd seen Kasavuvu do. I gazed helplessly through the openings in the wall as waves of displaced persons bound their mats and mattresses on their heads. They trekked down the long and winding road in front of the college to an unknown destination.

It was September and I had flown into Kinshasa to search for the philosopher's stone. I wore a neat Nigerian shirt with embroidery and shades you could see when in proximity. Light glowed from my well-polished shoes and hot air puffed like distress signals from my mouth each time I spoke.

Laurent-Désiré Kabila was fat to the point of being chubby. His neck weighed against his shoulders like a child wearing his father's suit. His head was big, as were his eyes. His chest was stout. When I asked who he was, all I heard was that he was a hare-brained guerrilla chief who rose to prominence years ago and thrived as a trafficker-at-large somewhere in Eastern Africa. He had become president as I was processing my admission in Lagos.

Kabila's rise to power followed a brief and spectacular military campaign throughout the country that ousted Maréchal Mobutu Sese

Seko. He became the chum of world powers. His friends regularly tossed him into the presidential chair and called him "Mze".

Mze was having a bad time, and I could tell from the look of things – the watery eyes of the Kinois, the trembling lips that disclosed in quick flashes the buckteeth of the refugees – that he wanted, indeed needed, support. He had fallen out of favor with Kigali, Kampala and Washington, the powers that had made him king. They wanted his head. "Damn," he said in an alert voice. "I'm the president."

Mze wore diamond wrist watches, Quoddy crafted shoes, and a dark safari suit that advertised his time in the marquee. He looked like Fidel Castro in the 1980s. To hide his bald head, he wore a Nike cap that laid a shadow across his face. His dark eyes blinked above a considerable nose underlined by a kinky moustache. Unlike Maréchal – petite and squat – Mze was something of a giant, imposing. His belly was a swollen sack and his shoulders were broad, good for carrying his grandchildren during parades and at fairs. He laughed a lot. He liked war movies. He danced Makossa alone in his office, drank a lot of beer, smoked a good deal of cigarettes and lived a mysterious private life, which had something to do with why any woman could get up in Kinshasa and claim to be his wife.

At first, after I left home, my father would e-mail whenever he could. He would tell me about the humidity in Lagos, the transitional program in Nigeria, Obasanjo's nomination as presidential candidate, my brother's medical school final exams, my sister's wedding, and the endless list of funerals. He would tell me how sound he was, how very sound. Then the e-mails came less frequently. Weeks of silence passed between them. Sometimes on the computer, I would type, "stop, stop, *stop* the massacre," hoping someone was reading. In October, after the European community in Kinshasa had fled the country through "Opération Malachite", I received an e-mail that read: "Hi Angelo. We're fine. News from Zaïre is disturbing. You can cross over to Brazzaville. Do your French homework. Love, Dad."

I printed it out and hung it on the wall with a slice of Scotch tape. I seriously considered heeding my father's advice, but Kasavuvu, who turned out to be my French teacher, convinced me to stay back in Kin-la-belle. He did not only teach me French under the gunfire, bullets, bombs and rockets that pulsated our days, but also techniques of self-defense in time of war. One morning Kasavuvu hammered my elbow so hard I couldn't raise my arm for a week. Another time I knocked one of his kidneys and he peed water. We struck each other with such force and frequency our knuckles blistered and blood came out like teeth through a squeezed lip.

The rebels, backed by Uganda and Rwanda, failed to capture Kinshasa. They withdrew eastwards to Kivu, the land overflowing with gem diamonds and other minerals. There, the brunt fighting went on. Soldiers had left the capital, but some soldiers remained in the city.

There were old officers the same age as my father, who lived close to the Jesuit College. These were Generals who had honored the fatherland, who had worked their jobs and fought their wars and now spent their days at the cantonment, drinking Belgian soup, complaining about the rogue generals, and arguing about a sergeant's beer pay. And they were untroubled. Rarely shaving, they relished listening to *Radio France Internationale*. These were men who lived in turfs and filled their shopping lists with Cheese Président, French sausage, Congar Cigars.

And then there were the opportunists like Eddy Nkunda, a man who scavenged whatever the refugees had left behind and visited homes of young women whose husbands had gone to war. Eddy had big ears and diminutive eyes and wore his hair in your standard-issue high-and-tight jingle. He spoke in a too-loud voice about all the rebels he gunned down when he manned a Katanga patrol unit. He lived in a bush outside Kinshasa, but spent his days in the capital strolling the parking lots of Mobil, Woodin', Casino, Ecomarché, ShopKo, On The Run, Israeli Embassy, and Alliance Française. He was looking for people like me, people whose appearance showed they were foreigners – or, better, enemies.

I didn't fully understand the reason several African nations were fighting in the

Congo. I only understood the Congolese crises had metamorphosed from a simple insurrection to Africa's World War, so they *had* to fight. The 'must' made the 'why' irrelevant. "It's all part of the game," my philosophy professor said. "American allies and

European corporate interests set the genocidal Congolese engine in motion." I could only cross my fingers and hope on luck and type "stop, *stop*," hoping the Congolese genocide would become part of Washington's political discussion.

One day, I walked down to the University of Kinshasa. There, near the dilapidated

Belgian-styled entrance, stood Eddy Nkunda. He wore his rugged khaki uniform and spoke with a group of other soldiers. They were laughing, shaking each other's hands as if they had had a good deal. I greeted them gently and they seemed to ignore me. I was unsure what would happen to me. When I was lucky, the troops manning the checkpoints would be sober. When I was not, then I just hoped my paperwork was in order, and that the weapon slung over the shoulder of the soldier trying to squeeze another dollar out of me, was pointing away from my brains – especially when the gunman was probably just thirteen.

"Question for you, gentleman," Nkunda said in the voice of a tired Congolese musician. "Can I have your IDs?"

I pulled off my bag with a flourish, my face feeling hot. "Here they are," I said, and forced a smile."

He took the bunch, opened them, looked at them and shook his head in disapproval. "You haven't got the AFDL permit. Anyone without the AFDL permit is a Banyamulenge,

Congolese Tutsi."

That word sent an inflammatory shock down my spine. "What?" I asked. "I'm not

Rwandan, I'm a Nigerian." He moved his gun. I grimaced even as I spoke along to soften his nerves. "I'm a philosopher not a rebel. I'm a friend of the Congo."

Eddy Nkunda's mouth tightened into a slight line, his posture uncurled, and he asked me what I thought Mze Kabila would think, hearing me right now. "We're risking our lives, gunning down the rebels, fighting Africa's World War I, and you're here *philosophing*," he said. "I think you're sick." His hand went out before him and into my pocket, one after the other. His fingers gripped all the Congolese francs in my pockets and he swiftly shoved them into his. "That's the best AFDL permit," he said, smiling.

I asked, "And can I leave now?"

"Right."

Exams came. All the professors waxed burly on the philosophy of violence and the just war theory. The world at the Jesuit College stood in sharp contrast to the chaotic, war-shattered country I lived in. I threw on my coveralls and wrenched on my studded boots and drove our deadbeat 4x4 Toyota with Kasavuvu to the villages of eastern Congo. Our tires kicked up dust and dirt and on sharp turns made cracking sounds. The bleating engine filled the eerie silence of the afternoon that had replaced the natural Congolese effusiveness before it crashed, forcing us to drag our Toyota behind us with towropes into the war-torn province.

Dense, garbage-heaped slums stretched for miles. Choking odors from the mass tombs rolled over our noses. Roads were cratered with potholes and ruts. Vicious militias and foreign armies roamed the jungle. Peddlers and refugees rushed up to vehicles stalled in steep potholes. We were in DR Congo's diamond hub, smack-dab in the middle of mineral reserves called a geological scandal. "Eastern Congo should glitter..." Kasavuvu said and appeared to have lost himself. I tapped his arm and he added, "Instead, it rots." I was exhausted and reeked of dirt, but I empathized.

"The bones shall rise someday, Kasa," I said.

In our house were people who had fled the fighting in the mountains of Haute Zaïre to join their relatives for safety. The house, a four bedroom flat, was over-crowded and about to collapse. Thirty people lived there. Clean water was insufficient and food was scarce. The occupants wore the same clothes everyday. Many were squalid, their only possessions being blankets and mats. They preferred to bear the obscurity than expose themselves to the M-16s of gory rebels.

Later, for lunch, we were served "chikwangu", Congolese "fufu," and sauce of cassava leaves. Our eyeballs glazed with heat, our ears roared with dry wind and our stomachs rose into our throats as we crashed down and felt like refugees. We began the slow trip through these thatch-roofed villages in the hills of eastern Congo.

I wore a coverall, armed with pen and paper, and with Kasavuvu ascended through a rutted, meandering path to the war-tattered villages up in the hills. It took several hours. The air had begun to go plum with evening when we stood at the lip of the void. I was sweating in my coverall as we smelled the wreckage of a destroyed village through the fog of our breath. I was conducting research for an article for a French journal. Suddenly I had a glimpse of chaos and poverty that encapsulated the DR Congo war. The villagers took what resembled a bundle of rags out of the thatch-roof hut to my right and laid it on the ground. But it wasn't a bunch of rags; it was a woman dying of starvation. She lay there as scraggy as a broomstick. She seemed conscious and stared at us with bright eyes. When a villager moved her, she screamed in agony, for her buttocks were covered with ulcerating bedsores. I said, "You better get her to a hospital or she will die." I shook my head in distress.

Kasavuvu said, "Just a few thousand Congolese francs and her life would be saved."

"They have a local hospital here," I said, and he added, "There's even the Catholic

Refugee Service somewhere around."

My words fell on deaf ears. The villagers stood still before a human being who would surely die if they didn't act. Kasavuvu rushed forward and put the woman's hands back in their former position before her cry of woe. There was nothing special about the woman except that she was dying in front of us. In villages throughout the eastern Congo, people like her had died by the millions from a lethal mix of war and poverty. The woman screeched again in what erupted as a gasping noise that sent me staggering back a few steps.

On the news, the Angolan troops were squashed after a brutal fight. On the news, Tanzania and Zambia had sent troops to support the rebels. South Africa supplied weapons and cash. Mze accused America of funding the rebellion. We climbed onto our Toyota and returned to the Jesuit College the way we came.

The warlords fought the Congo wearing bellicose boots. They fought Congo so much its wounds never had an opportunity to heal and its visage took on an unending look of decay.

Its wrists were swollen, its knees cramped, its joints suffered from dry wasps. They fought it until fighting ruined too much and they took up drinking *Primus* beer. Blood bags formed beneath the eyes of the sons and daughters of the Congo. Their shoulders ached; crinkles encircled their mouths like brackets.

Then came the news of Mze's assassination in his office by one of his bodyguards. An army chief trumpeted there were enemies in the land. Kinshasa came to a halt. Forces loyal to Mze haunted us on the streets, in the stores, on the highways, in the skies, everywhere. I tuned into the local TV and on display was Joseph, the twenty-nine year old former guerrilla fighter son of Mze, being installed as Congo's leader, thus making him the world's youngest head of state. He dived into the political limelight. He wore military fatigues and nodded repeatedly and said in a soft, publicity-naive voice, "I thank you." He closed his month and crawled away from the zoom of intrusive journalists. I pointed my finger at the show and said, with enough surprise in my voice to break a shocker, "See Congo and scatter."

When next I saw Joseph, he had swapped his grungy guerrilla uniform for a smart business suit. The moon shone down and dry harmattan wind blew from the north as we witnessed the burial of Mze. For a moment, just for a moment, the rascal generals put down their guns, and were unexpectedly sane. Just for a couple of minutes. Kasavuvu whispered into my ear in a slurred voice, "Mze was an obstacle to peace in the Congo. Now is time to step back and find a truce." He envisaged that peace had returned, abruptly.

Unexpectedly, Joseph's eye and mine caught each other from where he sat beside his mother. I had forgotten myself, staring off into the vast basin of the crammed Martyrs' Stadium where we had gathered to pay last tributes to Mze. It was hopeful and scary.

"Joseph will last long in power if they don't kill him," I said. "He has favor in America's eyes."

"Free me," Joseph seemed to respond to me, his voice cracking. He began to imagine. "Oh help. Don't. Please. The troubles of this vast battleground will worsen my bald head."

Hearing his great quivering sobs didn't help my condition. I knew decisions about the Congo would not be taken at the presidency, the "Palais de Marbles", but by European and American business moguls and mining magnates who roamed Lubumbashi, the Congolese mining capital. If anything, I felt as I did that day, so long ago, when Boyoma asked me to pay a hundred dollars or something to enter the Congo.

I was still lost in thoughts when, with a sudden lurch, the scoundrel generals ordered their militias to resume fighting in the eastern regions, a sad reminder that "The Kabila Boys" would have no control over large parts of the country.

I am a DR Congo war survivor. The messy war woke me up from my geopolitical slumber. It furnished me with a seeing eye and a speaking pen. It taught me to write about Africa from a balanced pen point: "Ready?" I wrote. "One!" Leopold II of Belgium, who started the European nations' "scramble" for territory in Africa, proclaimed himself King-Sovereign of the Congo Free State. Rubber brought great wealth to Leopold and Belgium; harvesting the crop inflicted terrible hardships upon the Congolese. "Set?" I wrote. "Two!" Congo's rebel commanders, dressed in expensive costume, massacre their fellow citizens just for power. *"Three."* I write. "Go!" Five million-plus skeletons lay on the DR Congo's grounds, but as long as the carnage is of benefit to a few Western allies, no holler.

I screwed the top onto my pen, put it into my bag, braced up and headed off to the N'djili Airport. After a random search that got my wallet missing, I quietly waited for the airplane to depart. When, at last, it pointed its nose at the thin air, I was filled with enormous relief, and I shouted, "I love you Congo, I LOVE YOU." I left the Congo knowing that *"la lotta continua"*, the struggle continues. And will continue.

Chapter 10

CATTLE RAIDING IN SOUTH SUDAN AND THE SHADOW OF WAR

Skye Wheeler

This is peace:
The chiefs and all sorts, too, have gathered in a thick ring around the beast. Foot-stamping, movement that is the beginning of dance. Within, there are discussions on how to do the ceremony. Blessed water is thrown into the air where it catches the sun. Ululations. Especially loud from the woman who seemed unhinged yesterday as she danced under the mango trees while the President spoke.

The top of the ring of people is filled with hats. Every chief has a hat; also a stick and wrinkles. People who have lived in war all their lives look different. There is the smell of alcohol at regular intervals in the packed conference tent of flamboyant red material. Almost everyone here is over six feet tall. Patient, long legs stretched out, the chiefs listen. After so much violence there is violence, they say, blowing fiercely on the microphone before they talk.

"You are killing yourselves," South Sudan's President Salva Kiir said the day before with sudden, evident frustration. "The liberation struggle is over. Why are we still killing ourselves?"

Through the backs and backs of legs, white eyelashes. Long lashes of the small white bull tethered to the ground with a beautiful, worn fork of wood. Its ears have been prettily crenellated. The drum is being beaten. The bull is the color of a cloud. Everything else is green and brown or is the river or the world-sized blue sky. Its head is brought to the ground, the horns twisted roughly, pushed into the earth, so the throat is upside. The eyes are rolled backwards. By the end, the position is so awkward the animal looks somehow like a large, bound dog.

Even as the blood runs out onto the ground the tail flicks in a panic. People are already dispersing as a herd of bleating goats run into the proceedings, breaking up the last of the ring.

The giant stomach is like a wet plastic shopping bag shaking in the wind. It is moved to show the big cavity. And then they start cutting between the hind legs like a birth, releasing bits of poop. A few minutes later the sternum has been roughly axed: the animal butterflied. The stomach bag is punctured and, as the six or seven people doing this work all expect, a lot of green fluid runs out. The cuts are distributed, and individuals walk into the tall grass with a leg or ribs over their shoulders. There is only the head, blood and grass-guts pool left and a pajama pile of skin.

Even before the cow has been cut in half and taken off into the grass in parts, most of those in the ring have dispersed back into the tented conference hall where a South Sudanese man who grew up in Australia is singing.

A man walks over to the remnants, takes the head by the horns and hoists it up onto his shoulders. He takes off down the narrow path between walls of seven-foot green like a small and barefoot Minotaur.

*

"It is a very special ceremony, rarely done," rebel commander-peace worker-humanitarian-businessman-sometime politician acquaintance of mine explained. "They cut the bull in half." He shows with one giant hand at a right angle to the other that lies flat, being sawed at. He has a big and mysterious grin, is well over six-foot and very black. We have pressed our arms against each other and laughed. Hairless black next to motley sandy white. He drives at over 100 kilometers an hour in the pitch black bush. I have asked him questions about violence, the war, polygamy, mined battlefields and cattle dowry. We, the other journalists and I who have been invited to cover the conference, all do everything he says, like helping with setting up chairs and tables. I suspect he has been proved, in that special mystical sense, beyond doubt. The war is still at the centre of him. It makes him very powerful. I try and learn as much as possible from him. But like everybody here, he is deeply biased on different levels.

*

While he is certain that the rebels won the war against northern Sudan, most would see the peace deal as a series of concessions on both sides. Khartoum controls the oil fields it sold off and developed in the South and has all the pipes and refineries. Southerners often talk about how they sold in their oil for peace. Observers say the north-south war, mainly fought in the wilds of the South, was un-winnable by either side.

On 9 January 2005 the rebel Sudan People's Liberation Army/Movement (SPLM/A) signed a Comprehensive Peace Agreement with Khartoum. The rebels also won 28 percent of seats in the national assembly and head up the South's semi-independent government, funded with its 50 percent share of oil revenues generated in South

Sudan. The SPLA became the South's official army and is struggling to transform itself from a massive voluntary force to a conventional one.

North-south tension has remained high and fighting has broken out twice between the two armies. This is the interim period. In 2011 the South will be able to choose whether to secede or not in a referendum. Under the deal, both signatories agreed to try and make unity attractive but most Southerners say they are just holding on, waiting, for independence.

*

The cow cutting is a second part of a peace deal between the Aguok and the Apuk, two clans from the South's large Dinka people that have been locked into a cycle of raiding and counter-attacks for years, killing hundreds and displacing whole villages.

This kind of murderous cattle rustling is common in much of the South: despite the peace agreement there is constant violence. Attempts at community disarmament have been mostly unsuccessful and occasionally disastrous with many more dead for a handful of AK-47s.

Cattle raiding has been part of Sudan's pastoralists' lives for generations. But, before the war, it was done with spears. Fewer cows were taken, many fewer lives. But with the last 21-year long civil war the South filled with thousands of guns. With greater capacity to hand, the number and the impact of the attacks increased. The usual methods of inter-community deals and peace-making began to fail and now the power of young people and ex-rebels with guns overshadows the authority of the chiefs. Their systems survive but like a skeleton; the war has washed the meat off. They supported the rebels, providing food and soldiers. The chiefs say they were promised that after the war they would get their judicial powers back. In the war, the rebels shot people for stealing a chicken.

Chief Makom Majong Makom's grandfather and father were both spearmasters. The spirit power, he said, has been passed to him even though his authoritarian realities are different. In his grandfather's time the spearmaster only had to tell off a member of his community and the bad act would never be repeated. Now Makom – who like many more senior chiefs, is also a court president - wants jails and the Dinka Wanh Alel customary law re-written so that it's much harsher. The most common kind of case he sees are cattle raiding ones.

Journalists tend to stick to South Sudan's capital Juba or to the capitals of its ten states. It takes a lot of time and money and often a small airplane to move around. One journalist working with the UN peace-keeping mission radio did see "tens of bodies lying on the ground". Ninety-five corpses were counted after that attack, although it is assumed the true death total is higher as some of the dead would have been carried back home.

As a result, although it is much talked-about, cattle raiding as a reality for rural peoples is under-explored. It remains a dark cast upon the new peace.

*

Local officials estimate that maybe 2,000 people have been killed in Warrap State cattle-raiding violence since the 2005 peace agreement. It may be an exaggeration but those who live and work there say it's probably not far off. Some people would call the hundreds and hundreds dead and injured per year a war in its own right, a researcher for the Small Arms Survey, James Bevan, pointed out on the telephone from Geneva.

Some youth from the near-by Kuac Ayok clan have recently got involved in the conflict and their chiefs too were included in the first part of the peace ceremony.

This involved the chiefs all putting their hands into a too-small half calabash held by Kiir's wife and two important widows of very important rebel leaders in South Sudan's long insurgency against Khartoum. Water was sprinkled onto the chiefs by the widows who, Kiir says, will curse those who break the accord they are taking part in.

The key to this peace is forgiveness. Everything then has to be forgotten, buried, so everyone can live better. The victims have to forget their revenge, their justice, even the loss of their children and livelihoods. It is hard to understand if you have not lived in war, takes a while to truly accept that fairness is often not possible, sometimes not necessary. After the ceremony there can be no more retribution for acts in the past.

But these agreements, countless numbers of them often made in conferences funded by international NGOs working in peace building, have often been broken just weeks after they are made.

"This has spilled over to your culture," Kiir said in his long speech to the chiefs. In this fragile peacetime, everyone is grabbing he added. In past times Dinkaland cattle raiders were treated like other criminals. But now it is becoming a part of being a man, a normal way to get rich. Growing surplus sorghum and other food and exchanging for animals, marriage, breeding: these used to be the ways to increase your wealth, the Southern President said.

"All they know is war, they were born into it," Kook Mawein, who grew up in America as a refugee said. Those who have returned after having left as children are often, like him, in their early or mid-thirties already. It was a long war.

In Dinka society, the cow is wealth, status, food source. Cows are central to most aspects of the culture. Young Dinka men must get cows from their relatives to marry. They are precious in themselves, but also in the centre of criminality in much of the South because they're just like money.

They also walk, Mawein continues. This is important when everything else you can invest in, like buildings or businesses or crops, can be easily destroyed in their place by conflict. And it's not yet certain that the war is truly over.

The possibility of war starting again is soaked into everything we journalists write about: new business development, disarmament, north-south relations, banking, agriculture.

The story is the interim period between war and the self-determination of referendum, a decision by the South on their fate. Living and writing in South Sudan is traveling in time between the two. That the stories are red with political tensions and further bloodshed may not be surprising to anyone. But they are also covers. Reporting the news covers the darkness behind the highly strung peace. When it breaks, when fighting breaks out, there is a sense of released tension. The obsession with the north and the constant focus on north-south relations may be necessary, but it also means Southerners have not yet had to truly address their own problems at home.

The story is written around a giant sleeping elephant in the room. No one knows what it will do when it wakes up. There is a lot of oil, potentially, in the South. Many don't believe Khartoum will give it up easily.

Mac Maika is a media expert working for the Association of Media Development in Southern Sudan, an umbrella organization that is, among other things, trying to get protective legislation for journalists passed in the South. There are many reasons why, as a group, we are weak. There is little money, little advertising, little equipment and poor infrastructure and not much by way of training. There is fear. One editor who has published stories on high officials and graft has been jailed twice. People, including body guards and officials, show signs of imbalance from war trauma and are unpredictable.

But there is also a strong sense that the environment is too fragile for journalists to really do their work, even if we really knew how to; it is not only government journalists that don't want to betray the South's slip-ups to Khartoum.

"It's just that the guns have stopped," Mac said. The other political parties don't put up any real fight. Corrupt politicians are maintained for harmony. No one wants to rock the boat.

*

Experts often point to this wider lack of security as one crucial reason why pastoralist inter-ethnic peace deals fail. Restorative justice is not just about forgiveness, it has to be practical too. Peace has to be believable.

*

A friend of mine, another journalist, thinks violence is natural and part of the spiritual history and future of the place, the South. More blood will be shed for the destiny of his South to be realized, he is sure, between the South's different peoples perhaps as part of getting freedom from the north.

Both my friend and I often write about death. Ten here and twenty-two there. Once almost a hundred in one attack. Children, women. It has become boring, little more than some words around a number, and I rarely get more than four or five paragraphs for a cattle rustling story now.

"Well, I am doing a cattle-raiding story. Twenty-two dead," I said to a TV journalist recently arrived in the South from South Africa looking for stories. Confused and assuming I meant the cows, he asked what was so interesting about how they had died.

*

From the small charter airplane Warrap State looks peaceful. It is a flat, endless green of scrub and *toich*, the wetlands that cattle keepers rely on during the dry season. It is this time of year that the body count racks up as cattle camps come closer together around the *toich*, also in short supply.

There's little sign of life until we start to descend over the small town of Tonj, built against the gentle Tonj River that has split into several different streams. The South is so flat that even the River Nile slows and breaks up like a delta. Some Southern refugees fresh from Ethiopia, I am told, expressed considerable distress at its hills.

Much of the South seems this empty. U.N. estimates put the population of the region at maybe 10 million. There are at least that many cows, perhaps two or three times as many, a U.N. Food and Agricultural

Organisation report said. South Sudan probably has the world's highest cows per people ratio in the world.

We are taken in a maroon bus from the airport to the buildings where we are to sleep. Everywhere it is green from the rains.

There are a few homesteads built alongside the road, under the giant and old colonial mango trees. Each is three or four huts with swept ground around them. These huts are dotted around the ruins of a giant jut factory that used to be here. Huge halls remain, open aired with only the metal frame of a roof remaining over the new acacia trees and weeds. Giant piles of machinery lie together, covered in grass that is also growing like flames along the tops of walls of the little stone houses where the jut workers used to live.

The conference was supposed to start on Monday after Kiir arrived, but he wanted to rest, so we waited, walked through the tall stalks of sorghum to the river for a swim.

In the evening, I interviewed Executive Chief Madut Aguer Adel, Tonj East. He is ancient-looking and bitter, although he also smiled kindly at me for the rest of the conference. He has fifty-four wives, including Aluk Kolinyin who is round-cheeked and excitable next to his old thin-ness. She has a big, friendly laugh. He is in despair: thousands of his community's cattle have been raided by neighboring groups. His community was disarmed, leaving them especially vulnerable.

"Many of our youth have gone to the town to get jobs because there is no cattle life now. These jobs are very miserable like cutting grass, or building or being waiters in the hotels. This is not the kind of work I would want them to do. I consider they have joined the town. It is a waste," he said.

The numbers he gives of people dead and cows taken are drastic. Afterwards, while we walk through the quiet gardens and huts of Tonj town from the school where the chiefs are sleeping, I ask my translator if he thought the numbers were an exaggeration. "I think they were an exaggeration," he said, smiling. I am used to this. After years of humanitarian aid, numbers of hungry, flood-affected, sick in cholera outbreaks, are often doubled by rural officials. The only mortality numbers that are not exaggerated are from cattle raiding: nothing can be done, I suppose.

I don't include his 30,000, 50,000 herd numbers in the write-up of the interview. But when I write about Court President Makom for another article a few weeks later, I include his explanation of how he knows the spiritual power has been inherited by him: he survived a lion leaping up at his throat and a militia attack just as a great-grandfather survived being enslaved and transported to Europe only to make his way back to Warrap again at the end of his life.

I suppose that it will be read with irony and also enjoyed. But there, under the red tent of the conference hall where we conducted the interview during a break in conference proceedings, however little I fathomed, I did understand the literalness of what he was saying. Few of my readers would believe it straight-up. He was a very serious and intelligent man. If the "readers" had met him, in that place, I think they too would have understood the seriousness of this bloodline of specialness.

The white bull, the river. The ruined jut factory. After war especially, things are what they are and also have strong representative properties. "Everything spiritual ends in violence," my friend says, and the dank rainy season wetness of Juba at night is better understood and even darker.

Irony is often reserved for the north, for Khartoum's behavior. "They say they want to make unity attractive but they do this?" Under the peace, it seems that both sides are re-arming and moving things into position. Perhaps the elephant is stirring, perhaps that is the slight tremors we feel.

*

There are other destroyed places like the jut factory in the South, a fruit cannery in Wau, for example. A bus for workers at a shut tobacco factory in Juba is still seen driving around the capital on entirely mysterious missions. The universities and most of the hospitals are in desperate need of rebuilding and renovation. I interviewed a lab technician at the University of Juba as he meticulously washed, one by one in soapy water, test tubes, racks, beakers that had been locked away for decades while the north-south war raged. There were also twenty year old bottles of iodine and vials of other chemicals with rubber stoppers. "They may still work," he said, smiling.

*

As President Kiir often says, the point of peace for the South is not to rebuild or renovate but to start building. More than 50 years of north-south peace, with only a ten-year gap in between two wars, has left the South drastically under-developed, decades behind its neighbors. It has the world's highest rates of maternal mortality. Only 25 percent of the population has any access to healthcare and many children die before they are five years old.

In October 2005 the SPLM set up its government in the new capital of Juba, a garrison town controlled by Khartoum for all of the war despite the best efforts of the rebels. With the oil cash flowing and the humanitarians arriving in droves, the town quickly gained a reputation as East Africa's boom town and hundreds of entrepreneurs from around the region and the world set up hotels and import businesses, fuel stations and Chinese restaurants.

But importing generators can hardly be described as investing and the hotels are mostly tented camps or prefabs: no one is prepared to invest fully with the risk of a restart of the conflict.

*

Some 50,000 people were displaced from the oil-rich Abyei area – claimed by both north and south - in the middle of the year. These internally displaced have mostly been displaced before. They were exhausted, thin and closed up but also immediately ready with the stories, probably mostly true but told without the newness of truth, for aid workers.

One young man's eyes seemed as dark as the purple sky – it was about to rain – as he talked to me. He said his wife had died in labor on the run. It may have been a lie. I used it in a story, anyway. Miserable and surrounded by broken up families trying to shelter in nooks in the suddenly people-flooded town of Agok, I decided it was good enough to be used, whatever that means. Over there, somewhere to the north, there were a dead woman and baby, and now his fury was also partly at me. I deserved it, of course. Further north, there had been a battle, one of the thousands on this flat land. I had not been there. I am asking my questions at the margin, where the displaced are crouching out of the rain under a broken roof. It's totally unacceptable, but as a journalist you don't say that, you describe it. Show, don't tell. The description is always less than it should be.

I am in the margin now of the interim period, after the peace deal. I am asking questions to the war-affected and then writing it all down, assuming that this is peacetime and that things are okay now.

There was a rawness to my bereaved source, and he seemed somehow amoral. Even his anger seemed something of an echo, used up. His story was probably a lie. I shouldn't have used it in the story. But what am I supposed to believe, having known only the margin? I haven't been in the war. I have just talked to the war-affected, and sometimes I feel I am in someone else's nightmare.

*

I asked an official from the state government about the White House, Juba's infamous torture house. "Why are you bringing these things up now? We don't want to speak about them," he said. He was angry, trembling. The next time he saw me it was all smiles and effusive greetings, forgotten.

*

Cattle-keeper Deng Thon spends the last half hour of daylight cleaning dung from the area around his beloved white bull that nonchalantly chewed cud at dusk. He works close to the ground, sweeping with his hands. Fires of dry cow dung have been lit to keep away the flies. It has been this way for a multitude of generations. The River Tonj is calm, slipping through the toich.

*

In an interview with the English paper, *The Guardian*, author Terry Pratchett explained why he quit journalism: because he hated asking people who had clearly suffered a serious loss how they felt. For the papers.

Poverty, a lack of options, education, the guns, the usual human desire for wealth: all these reasons for the never ending deaths for cattle have been documented, studied by analysts, NGO workers, humanitarians, government officials. The dawn surprise attacks on the cattle camps, the shooting: the punctured dead lying on the ground. There's very little description of the truth of how all of this is because, really, it's just too dark to see it.

Last year in Eastern Equatoria State, tens of women and children were gunned down in the fields where they were working. It was an inter-ethnic problem. No one knew what to say about this at all, really.

We report on this development or that, the journalists, struggling with the heat and the general disorganization and ambiguity. We write about new tensions between the north and south or the efforts to diffuse them, an outbreak of polio, telecommunications. It's all about the war really, or the fragility of the peace, this new status of being at peace. The five paragraphs on more cattle raiding death in some far-flung state.

No one asks too many questions, or pushes too deep. It's just too stupid to ask people how they feel sometimes, or even to examine it. The psychological impact of this war will probably not be felt until the real, final peace comes with independence, if it does. Then perhaps some will have the time and space to set aside politics for an evening or two and the real writing will begin.

Chapter 11

PREACHERS ON THE TRAIN

Munyaradzi Makoni

I wait, but the bus never comes. I sweat; my body becomes lame. I am edgy and agitated.

The rank attendant on the other side of the street later tells me I am standing on the wrong station. By then my mind has already traveled into another world, a mortal separation of body and mind. This is the beginning of a journey that I do not know how it would mould my identity, my career and my whole life.

I make a smile laced with embarrassment; I recall that I have not hugged my daughter goodbye in the morning. In a frenzied run, I cross six streets heading for her pre-school where I ask to see her. With a hearty hug I ask her what she would want me to bring her on my return. With childish innocence, she blurts out, some shoes daddy.

I have not gone back. I have not bought her the shoes. I am not sure if she still recognizes me. I now wear spectacles. I have gained a few kilos.

I think of it three months later on the third night of sleeping on the cold hard pavement with a cardboard for a mattress, a rain-drenched duvet for a blanket.

These are some of the times I feel disowned by a country that I am seeking safety from. I feel sorry for myself. What security is there when you have to watch your dignity being stripped down like a woman caught sitting in a mosque. I have almost become a permanent resident at the Foreshore in Cape Town. For some people it has become a permanent home, a home without an address. This is the same place where Adonis Musati, a former Zimbabwean policeman, died of hunger in November 2007 while waiting to get his visa. This is the pick-up point for people who are still to regularize their stay in South Africa. People driven by famine, genocide, bad economy, war and political persecutions from their mother countries.

I will always remember with a mixture of awe and sadness how I earned brickbats from my former employer during management meetings. I was quizzed several times to explain why there were not enough good things to say about the ruling party in our publication.

"Are you telling me you have no other things to lead your paper except to say Mugabe has killed the country?" It was an open prodding: do things our way.

The writing has been on the wall for some time, but I was not confident to read it. Each time my conscience said the hour had come, I would ask it, where do you want me to go? I have a family to feed. But the incubation had reached maturity stage. I had to face the facts.

The newspaper where I worked is credited as one of the publications that fought the liberation war. When it dies one day, it must be buried at the Heroes Acre. Not that I wish it dead, but I am desperate for people to recognize it for what it is and what it can still do. After independence, it fought for the voiceless. It championed the cause of human rights. Then somewhere along the line, it lost the agenda. It failed to live up to the expectations of its readers. However, the sting could be there. Once in a while it could raise the stink and the government henchmen would contort their faces: "Is this what you call news?"

But it had also become too erratic to be taken seriously. The print run had drastically gone down. The economic epilepsy that bogged down the printing industry had made everything unstable. In fact, the seizures had affected anything that involved money.

This is a personal assessment. I'm hesitant to go on sermonizing about political and economic problems. They have provided enough conversations. Zimbabwe is not a war zone but a country in a political and economic cesspit. It has broken all known inflation records. It has taken all the medals in humiliating its own people. One night you can find revelers gyrating to the fast-paced tunes of Alick Macheso at Circus Night Club in Harare. On another night you might find some people scampering for safety at Up Town nightclub in Gweru, soldiers beating them for disowning the party that delivered them from colonialism. It is called a human tragedy induced by power without conscience.

Well, I got sick of it. Sick of trying to convince myself that some miracle would deliver me from this national catastrophe. Sick of walking to work simply because I could not afford transport daily. Sick of waiting for a paper that never got printed on time. I got sick of writing for international publications under a pseudonym lest I got branded an enemy of the state. Sick of borrowing money and having to borrow again to pay back whoever had lent me in the first place. Sick of a nation that got into wacky debates on whether the president was the worst or best thing that ever happened to the country since the Union Jack was lowered on 18 April in 1980.

Preachers on the train

Far from being a celebrated writer in my own country and the prospects of achieving that status under the circumstances extremely remote, one bright summer morning, I fill a leave form. It is hesitantly signed. I tell myself: "Anywhere else besides Zimbabwe was better."

Please note, nobody held a gun to my head, but there are times when patriotism cannot buy a banana for your only child or maternity dress for your expecting wife or afford asthma medication for a distant aunt.

With these bits of information you might find resonance in my story. Maybe you understand now how I find myself on the wrong side of the bus station. How I become a face in the crowd among former teachers, policeman and women, soldiers, nurses mechanics and even beauty queens.

I still have a pen and a notebook, though, in my pocket.

A pen ceases to be useful when it cannot write. A writer stops to exist when he adopts disability and becomes deaf and dumb. I wrote words in my heart and mind. Somehow, I imagine myself as an unknown distant protégé of the late great Russian writer, Alexander Solzhenitsyn. Solzhenitsyn was forced to write books in his mind when Russian prison authorities denied him writing materials when he was their "guest."

Finding a job that feeds my passion has proved tough. But the annoying oddness of wearing a foreigner's tag irks me most. I think Africa should be one big village where we don't have to scramble for identity at every street corner. Being a foreigner, nobody thinks you can write a single grammatically correct sentence. Some of them look at you and pass an immediate judgment on your physical appearance.

Maybe, I have been looking in the wrong places. That's how I comfort myself several times.

It gets so bad that I decide to tell whoever wants to hire me that I am South African. If they swallow the bait and call me for an interview, I would tell them that I am an African from southern Africa. Technically that makes me a South African. A cheap trick, it has not worked.

Eventually, I got a job that sees me changing my name and growing in love with food. In the name of food I baptized myself Mark. Customers have problems with my name, so a corrupted version of my surname, I assume, would be ideal. The daily tension of survival costs eases though I can barely afford my most basic necessities. As I hold a docket book each night taking customers' orders, I fantasize about interviewing people for stories. For two nights in a row I dream of starting my own food publication in the new Zimbabwe. These acts keep the writer in me alive.

When daylight comes I settle for the real thing. I walk the streets looking for stories to sell.

Monetary rewards of a freelance writer trying to break the virginity of markets in a foreign country take long to mature. It becomes more depressing when you actually know the savings you left at home are dwindling. It's even worse when you don't have a computer, camera and a phone that works.

I nearly gave up. I reached the breaking point but somehow I did not break. It seems I waited for eternity before I received a single rand. This is despite managing to have a few stories published. I have to survive.

Back home they were impatient for the good news. The moment I crossed the border, they concluded, good times would roll. Little did they know I was yet to taste the honey or see the colour of the milk. I must give a token to whoever started the Internet cafes. They broke my monotony of boredom while providing me a desk and a computer. I cannot deny Telkom South Africa a card and some flowers either for generously putting telephone booths on the streets. I could always look for a secluded street to do a telephone interview to beat a deadline that never considered my circumstances.

I have heard people say, South Africa is a third world country with a first world economy. Who can deny it? The opulence of the rich in leafy suburbs in contrast to heart-breaking poverty in most black townships could literally make one weep. Tin shacks, drug abuse, AIDS-related deaths, cold-blooded violence and xenophobic attacks – that's all part of the other side of South Africa that gets edited out by the media. I became part of it. I developed a strong social conscience about these communities. There were stories of hope and aspiration that were never told about these people. I wrote some of them. I was mugged three times. I lost my battered phone and money. I was never angry. I call it 'nationalization'. They had taken from me to give to a brother or sister who did not have. I was only facing to something that is almost 'normal' in the country. Crime!

It strikes me that sometimes you are whatever you wear. One day I am wearing a T-shirt with a tooth-gapped image of Steve Biko, as I stand at the street market, hesitant and shy to rummage through male underwear tangled with female underwear in public view. My eyes rest on two ruffled novels under the trolley.

"*I write what I like,*" the vendor says, sharing her knowledge about Biko's most famous book. "*I like what I write,*" I respond. The taste of the rhyme on the tongue is so good. We start chatting.

Armani is originally from Rwanda. She claims to be a marketing graduate from the University of Cape Town. Given her depth of knowledge it could be true. She has tried fruitlessly to get a formal job, so she started her grocer-on-the wheels business.

"This is not my passion. I love books. I read lots of books. I wish I could break into writing," she says, sounding upbeat. We chat more about the hardship of writing. About the demands and rewards of writing. I promise to help. I wish I could help. I shelve the idea. Maybe one day I might help.

I am slowly living the dream against the odds. In my decade long career, my frustrations have fired my sharpest writing ever. I realize I cry for a job that I already have. The situation that drove me away from home has shaped my resilience. Money or lack of it keeps me sane.

I have always thought events in Africa have provided enough pitfalls on how not to run a country, so big countries like South Africa must not falter. I feel sore when it appears that the African National Congress (ANC) is reading from the same script as Zimbabwe African National Union (ZANU). ANC has failed to transform itself into a modern day political party that respects its country's constitution. Cronyism, patronage and corruption have become industries unto themselves. Some people say it's healthy for democracy. I do not buy the idea. Maybe it points to what journalists and writers must focus on deeply.

I remind myself that writing critically on the politics of a host country could land me back where I came from. Fear keeps me on the borderline. I don't have the mandate to tell South Africans what to do with their politics. Poking serious fun on authorities is one sure way to have your visa cancelled. I have never tried. I will not dare. I have set my sights on those - human interest - stories that are usually ignored in their humble form. Most recently I have found my taste for science writing sweet. I had never imagined while drinking one for the road in the comfy Golden Mile Hotel in Kwekwe that one day, I would discover writing about science interesting as much as it is intriguing.

So, life keeps moving. Despite occasional delays, putting my head in someone's stinking armpit when overloaded during peak hours, I have grown to love the metro trains. If someone could pay me to watch the drama that unfolds daily, listen to the whistling of illegal train vendors and digest the sermons from a deluge of preachers, I could take it. Some people only use the trains because they are cheap. I have grown to love the preachers too.

They preach about sex, human dignity, self respect and love. But some preachers are so daft. They can tell you that there is no God. Sometimes one cannot help taking pity on them. Sometimes the contradictions are so brazen that you listen and laugh. Laugh and listen. Some of the preachers are foreigners who came to seek for safety. Others are locals whose heavily accented Afrikaans English makes them unmistakable.

What amazes me is not the misinterpretation of the Bible. It is not the colour of their skin, neither is it their country of origin or words that refuse to come out of their mouths when they want to preach.

There is no difference between them and me. We share the same roles. I preach in my writings about survival, hope and aspiration on the train of life. They exhort people to follow the good route to life. Whether they manage to convert one or two souls, it does not matter. Alternatively, I do not know how many people read what I write. We are all preachers on the train, our destinations different, our wishes mingling. And departing.

I think the writer in me has survived relocation.

Chapter 12

THE JOURNEY HOME: SUITCASE OR COFFIN?

Lauryn Arnott

Artists are storytellers who communicate their stories by building up images from marks that are applied and layered onto paper or canvas. Artists use pens, sticks of charcoal or brushes loaded with liquid paint to create a visual language. As an artist, I am indebted to Africa by the fact that I have lived alongside a culture where art is not only made for ornament but serves the purpose of making a significant statement.

I believe that art, like storytelling, should serve the purpose of being associated with the same magic that our ancestors possessed when they first drew on cave walls the animals on which their survival depended.

The British artist and art writer, John Berger, was once asked if he thought that the position of *being* an outsider, a foreigner, could be a stimulus for making art? His reply was illuminating:

> Yes, it begins with storytelling. The storyteller is, equally, in the story and outside it. All art perhaps involves moving between one or two or several 'places.' You're inside what you're drawing, and you're outside the drawing, watching it. Simultaneously in two places. The artist is never in a single place - and in this he's like a foreigner, trying maybe to create a temporary home.

There is something about the sensibility of being foreign, a feeling of not being accepted or acceptable, which is most apparent when, as a woman, you arrive in the strange world of art where most of the citizens are men and where the fate of women has not been settled. As a white African, you are perceived as separate from your place of birth and the country of your origins. So, sometimes you are a double outsider, moving between one or two or several places at once. As an artist I find this existential condition a great source of creative inspiration and symbolic wealth.

My form of expression is drawing. My ability to draw gives me the opportunity to measure and articulate my experiences. Given the layers of difference and exclusion at birth, I draw to reconcile my memories that have been confined by race, gender, nationality and history. In my work I explore the body as more than surface and try to give form to those experiences, which take place in the margins between 'inside and outside'.

The method that I use when drawing is called pentimento. This term is derived from the Italian language and can be translated as: "to repent or to redeem." It is also a technical term that describes the approach of painting or drawing using the combination of erasure and addition. The drawing process is a technical way in which I can deal with themes of memory and loss. It is not only important what I draw but how I draw.

The pentimento method of drawing was almost like a physical enactment of the very state in which I found myself after I fled from Zimbabwe, my country that has been torn apart and demoralised by those who rule with chaos, madness and fear. It was not only my arrival in Australia, a land of safety and security that placed me in that condition, but my departure from Zimbabwe. The drawn mark became an element of retrieval, its erasure a metaphor of loss. This process was important for many reasons, not the least of which was the central need to mark a new place through the persistent memory which I brought, acknowledged and unacknowledged, to my new country.

In 1980, President Robert Mugabe, the hero of Zimbabwe's war of independence, declared Zimbabwe to at last be free from the yoke of colonial rule. In the year 2000, after twenty years of his democratic rule, he promised to correct the perceived land distribution in the country. In driving the white farmers out, Mugabe's campaign set out to vilify past transgressions done during the country's British colonial history and to vindicate the people of Zimbabwe.

However, the take-over of white-owned farms was the beginning of the displacement of all who opposed the president's "rule of law." He later ordered the destruction of 700,000 houses in which 2.4 million people lost their homes and their livelihood in what he called *Operation Murambabatsvina*, also known as "Operation drive out the trash."

The United Nations' reports declared that this method of using violence, as a political tool to brutalise and dehumanise the citizens of Zimbabwe, created a humanitarian crisis of immense proportions.

After the botched 2008 elections, people who did not vote for the ruling party were driven from their homes in "Operation Mavhoterapapi" also known as "Who did you vote for?"

Despite the continued official insistence that no violence was taking place in the country, Zimbabweans have seen life expectancy slip to one of the lowest in the world. Zimbabwe's world-record inflation rate has transformed a country that was once called a regional breadbasket into a space of grinding poverty and mass starvation.

Mugabe's "land and home take-overs" set a course of displacement, dire starvation and massive disenfranchisement that in turn triggered an exodus of one of Africa's most educated populations.

I too became part of this Diaspora of Zimbabweans looking for a better future for my children. I never lost Zimbabwe, as I never had it, for I was separated from it. I identified with the suffering and rage that the people experienced, separated by colonialism. I wait for the day when the citizens of Zimbabwe can leave the past behind and join the people across the world who have challenged and questioned Western cultural monopoly and can contribute towards the affirmative debates on post-colonialism, cross-cultural identities, and globalization.

I agree with a statement by Sam Njami, the curator of the Africa Remix exhibition of African contemporary art that is travelling across the globe:

> We are shaped by the places that we come from, we are products of the time that we live in, we are products of the places that we have lived, we are products of personal and global history, our objective as artists is to translate this into our work.

I feel encouraged by Njami's words to look beyond the present, as I consider creative artists who have infused their art with personal and historical experiences of living in times of conflict and who reflect on global issues that transcend barriers of race, colour, and religion. I am inspired by the work of the German artist Max Beckmann, who lived through a humanitarian crisis in his country. He did not choose the time or the place of his birth or to be classified German during Adolf Hilter's persecution of the German Jews. However, he chose to articulate and paint pictures in an attempt to convey and transcend the memory and guilt of the Holocaust. In this, his paintings conveyed stories about people living in a brutalised society and the memories that it leaves in its wake. Beckmann stated:

> Painting is a very difficult thing. It absorbs the whole man, body and soul – thus I have passed blindly many things that belong to real and political life.
>
> I assume, though, that there are two worlds: the world of spiritual life and the world of political reality. Both are manifestations of life that may

sometimes coincide but are very different in principle. I must leave it you to decide which is more important.

Thanks to Beckmann's influence, I discovered that I could express and "fix," through drawing, my fascination with and despair about the cultural ties that bind me to Zimbabwe and southern Africa. This helps me live with my conscience despite the historically brutal times under which I have lived. In the drawing process, using the pentimento technique, I photographed and documented twelve different stages. I drew, sanded, then redrew over the old memories, taking up only what was essential for my new life.

When I arrived in Australia from Zimbabwe I started on a large drawing that took two years to complete. It is called "Journey Home." In this drawing, I proceeded through many different stages to work through memories and feelings related to experiences of displacement and departure from Zimbabwe.

The boxes depicted in the drawing are associated with the constant moving and packing, which was necessary at different times of the strife and occasioned by the deaths of friends, opposition party members, farm workers, farmers, or people dying of starvation because it was unlawful for white farmers to grow food to feed the nation. I used newspapers to wrap up my belongings. These papers contained pictures and stories that hid or exposed the lives of ordinary black and white people, who displayed great courage because they did not believe in the madness that heralded a season in hell. I remember thinking that the crates that I was sending off were to be like time capsules that could tell everyday stories about the banality of evil that was nurtured to replenish hungry people during that bleak season of terror.

I promised myself that if I ever did find a safe distance I would use that gift, that luxury, to draw and to remap this journey, a journey taken to elude from those who wish to tear the world down. The journey I recreate is a movement undertaken by thousands upon thousands of people changing the future, on buses, airplanes, on foot, swimming across rivers, climbing fences, to become legal and illegal citizens in various lands of exile. That movement is akin to a rite of passage, a journey with no direction home, with a suitcase or in a coffin.

I watched people walking, walking with their lives in a cardboard box, walking no-where, walking anywhere, to a safe haven under the stars. The "Journey Home" drawing is about witnessing moments in history at the wrong or the right time, of being classified the wrong or the right colour, but it is essentially about what lies ahead and what is important for a new life. The legacies of these events have conditioned the transitions that have shaped this picture.

Before I completed the drawing my boxes arrived. The unwrapping and unpacking of familiar possessions in a new and strange land was a rite of passage that was both joyous and melancholic, as I recalled the loss and the relief. In this course, I looked within to see that I carry in my body a seed inherited from Eve, the original sin. On the outside I wear the colour of my inheritance, my forefather's skin.

The drawing, like my history, was a contested area. In its unmasking I had to enter into the paper by sanding and thus distressing the surface, creating rough fissured areas that evoke rawness. Through this I managed to achieve a luminosity and the "tooth" required to offer purchase to new marks on the surface.

I drew, then I erased, using sandpaper, then drew again. In sanding the paper, holes appeared, making it quite fragile and thin in areas. Through this I hope to comment on the fragility of human life and the vulnerability of peace in the countries of southern Africa. I do not wish to lay blame or demonise. I just hope that in laying bare these ideas we can penetrate the surface of our skins and discover that underneath we are all human and that life is holy, as it should be for the sake of our children.

The "Journey Home" won the 2006 Association of Commonwealth Universities Art Prize in a competition entitled *A Place in the World*. It was unexpectedly symbolic that the South African-born writer, J.M. Coetzee, who now resides in Australia, was invited to award the prize. It is also symbolic that the drawing now hangs in the London headquarters of the Association of Commonwealth Universities. As the drawing represents the Diaspora not only of Zimbabweans, irrespective of race or colour, but symbolizes the story of the many people who have been displaced by greed and conquest, I believe it has found an appropriate "home."

(see illustrations)

PHOTOGRAPHIC DOCUMENTATION OF LAURYN ARNOTT'S DRAWING TITLED *JOURNEY HOME*, FEBRUARY - DECEMBER 2004

The journey home: suitcase or coffin?

State 1, size:150 x132 cms next to the small working drawing

Lauryn Arnott

State 3, March

The journey home: suitcase or coffin?

State 5, April

Lauryn Arnott

State 7, May

State 9, November

State 12-final state, 31st December

Lauryn Arnott
Journey Home
2004
Charcoal and charcoal pencil on Dessin 200 gsm paper
150 x132 cms
Collection of the Association of Commonwealth Universities, London

PART TWO

REFLECTIONS AND CONVERSATIONS

Chapter 13

"LITERATURE ON DEMAND?" VIOLENCE AND THE LITERARY IMAGINATION IN CONTEMPORARY SOUTHERN AFRICAN FICTION IN ENGLISH

David Bell

In a recent interview, Zakes Mda, the well-known South African writer, was asked what influence the ending of apartheid had had on his literary output. In reply he stated:

> I am free now. And the end of apartheid has freed the imagination of the artist. I tell stories now. But these stories come from an environment that is highly politically charged. . . . But my main mission is to *tell a story, rather than to propagate a political message. During apartheid, it was the other way around.* It was part of my political commitment, I wrote plays. I only started novels after the political changes. (My emphasis)

Mda's position, that the emphasis for a writer must be on the literary imagination rather than on the propagation of a political message, is not new, as he has consistently argued that his own writing has been successful primarily because, as a writer living outside South Africa, he has been forced to use his imagination (Cf. Holloway). The stance taken by Mda echoes the debate that emerged in South Africa in the late 1980s on the role of culture in the struggle against apartheid. At that time Albie Sachs, among others, argued against "culture as a weapon in the struggle", "solidarity criticism" and "sloganeering".[1] It should be recognised, however, that this is not a new debate and neither is it one confined to South Africa. The polarisation between "art for art's sake" and "ardent propaganda" has a long history and both revolutionary movements and reactionary governments have been active in promoting reductive and proscriptive critical attitudes to literary works.[2] This does not mean that literary works should avoid social critique, but rather that it is in the spaces occupied by the creative imagination that literature can best bring to the reader new perspectives and new insights; there are other forums for propaganda and sloganeering.

Consequently, this chapter aims to illuminate how three contemporary novelists from southern Africa, Zakes Mda, the late Yvonne Vera and Sindiwe Magona, have used the freedom offered by creative writing not only to depict violence itself, but also to explore modes of redemption.[3]

In his work Mda usually generates a point of departure in a contemporary narrative which is linked to past events. In the case of *Ways of Dying* (1995), the contemporary story is the meeting and reconciliation of the former home-village antagonists, Toloki and Noria, in the week between Christmas and New Year. The novel maintains the ideological themes that have been apparent in Mda's work since his early plays—the struggle against apartheid and the betrayal of the revolution through corruption and neo-colonial practices. He also makes use of the creative act of drawing as an ameliorative process which leads to a better future.

Ways of Dying was based on the reports of violence Mda found in South African newspapers available at Yale University—the *City Press* and the *Sunday Times*—in the first few months of 1993 and supplemented by other firsthand accounts. The novel focuses on the violence that was prevalent in South Africa between 1990 and 1994 and is an unsentimental study of gratuitous violence. The two key scenes in the novel, those of the necklacing of an eight-year old boy and the massacre of the inhabitants of an informal settlement, are described in close detail:

> Danisa's match fell into Vutha's tyre. It suddenly burst into flames. His screams were swallowed by the raging flames, the crackle of burning flesh, and the blowing wind. ... Soon the air was filled with the stench of burning flesh. (189-190)

> In one shack, a woman who was nine months pregnant was stabbed with a spear. As she lay there dying, she went into labour. Only the head of the baby had appeared, when it was hacked off with a panga by yet another warrior. (182)

Other violence, ranging from domestic quarrels to taxi wars, permeates the novel, leaving the impression that this is the normal state of affairs. As readers, we are not unaffected by this all-pervading violence, and the use of a communal narrator demands complicity not simply in the narrative but as witnesses to the events—no-one can deny knowledge.

While the violence in *Ways of Dying* can be traced to specific reports, the story itself has no named geographical location. Mda's setting is an unnamed city with all the hallmarks of Johannesburg, or Durban or Cape Town. In effect, violence in *Was of Dying* is violence in South Africa as a whole. With Toloki's, the male protagonist's, story told in flashbacks, the catalogue of violence is extended over a period of 30 years and becomes, thereby, historically conditioned. The two qualities of anonymity and historical recurrence turn the ever-present violence in *Ways of Dying* into the state of the nation.

The problem with this image is, of course, that violence, both historically and particularly in the 1990-1994 period, was not as universal as Mda's novel would suggest. The recorded violence of the early 1990s period was by-and-large confined to the Gauteng and KwaZulu/Natal provinces where the struggle between the African National Congress (ANC) and The Inkatha Freedom Party (IFP) was at its most intense, and where informal settlements became sites of the struggle for political control. In 1993, 2,009 people died in this conflict in KwaZulu/Natal alone and between 1992 and 1993, 90% of taxi deaths were in KwaZulu/Natal and Gauteng, which represented a doubling in numbers – to name but a few examples.[4]

However, *Ways of Dying* goes beyond the documentation of violence and seeks a form of salvation and redemption in mutual, human kindness and the creative energy of individuals in a community. In the week between Christmas and New Year, which is the time span for the main story, Noria and Toloki find mutual respect in each other. Noria learns from Toloki's humility how to live and from Noria, Toloki learns self-respect and sociability. To these human needs are added imaginative, creative qualities, such as those expressed in the rebuilding of Noria's shack into a wonder of many colours, and the furnishing of it with pages torn from interior design magazines. In a leap of imaginative faith and literary skill, Toloki and Noria are able to momentarily experience a life of luxury in their bare, one-roomed, earthen-floored shack (112-114). Equally, Noria helps Toloki to re-discover his skills as an artist and this enables him to release the joy and creativity of the children of the settlement.

> Children stop their games and gather around him. They watch him draw colourful pictures of children's faces. The children from the dumping ground and the settlement are able to identify some of the faces. . . . They laugh and make fun of the strange expressions that Toloki has sketched on their purple and yellow and red and blue faces. (199)

The message is clearly, if sentimentally, one of hope. If the past sees institutionalised violence, the future sees a humanist, mutual, creative understanding.

The main protagonists in Yvonne Vera's *The Stone Virgins* (2002) are two sisters, Thenjiwe and Nonceba, who come from a small, country town and become the innocent victims of the political differences that arise between the dissidents and the government after independence. Cephas, a librarian from Bulawayo, becomes involved in their fate. Yvonne Vera's prose has been described as poetic and lyrical, but despite this, her description of events in Matabeleland gives a clear and intimate picture of the effects of violence on the individual – the fright, fear, shock and insult that it means.[5] Thenjiwe's execution is told in 'slow-motion' as it is seen and experienced through Nonceba's eyes. Thus, it cannot be simply an objective observation, a distant gaze, it is full of Nonceba's perception, response and amazement at what happens.

> "Thenjiwe . . ." she calls. A man emerges. He is swift. Like an eagle gliding.
>
> His head is behind Thenjiwe, where Thenjiwe was before, floating in her body; he is in her body. He is floating like a flash of lightning. Thenjiwe's body remains upright while his man's head emerges behind hers, inside it, replacing each of her movements, taking her position in the azure of the sky. He is absorbing Thenjiwe's motions into his own body, existing where Thenjiwe was, moving into the spaces she has occupied. Then Thenjiwe vanishes and he is affixed in her place, before Nonceba's eyes, sudden and unmistakable as a storm. The moment is his. Irrevocable. His own. ...
>
> How does a man slice off a woman's head while a bucket was carried above it? How did a man slice a woman's throat and survive? ...
>
> What did he use to cut Thenjiwe's head off, so invisibly, so rapidly? (73, 74)

Through Nonceba's thoughts and eyes, questions are raised about male power and violence, in particular, violence to women. In her perception of the event, Sibaso replaces Thenjiwe; he becomes the holder of power: "The moment is his. Irrevocable. His own." However, a deep moral issue is raised in the question Nonceba poses about her sister's murder, "How did a man slice a woman's throat and survive?", as it questions not only the act of murder, but emphasises it as a breach of a moral code punishable by death - a punishment to be enacted automatically by some avenging force. The reader's experience of this cold-blooded act is reinforced by the sensation of how Sibaso, the deranged "dissident" and Thenjiwe's murderer, slices away Nonceba's lips:

...just a fleeting touch is all she feels, not lasting except the incessant pain afterwards. She thinks it is just that, his touch along the chin; instead, it is razor sharp. . . .His motion was simple. It was soft and almost tender, . . .I felt nothing. He sought my face. He touched it with a final cruelty. He cut smoothly away. He had memorized parts of me. Shape and curve; lips unspoken. (79)

This mutilation is described almost as an act of love with caresses and soft, sensuous movements that hide a surgical, inhuman incision.

Details of barbarous behaviour are also a stylistic device used in the account of what is intended to be a description of the 5 Brigade's progress through the village. By juxtaposing the cruel execution of the village storekeeper with the soldiers' emotionless behaviour, Vera makes the reader aware of the brutality suffered by civilians in Matebeleland between 1982 and 1987. Equally, she formulates her tale in such a way that the reader is unavoidably left with a sense of guilt:

Mahlathini, long the storekeeper of Thandabantu Store, has died. Those who claim to know inch by inch what happened to Mahlathini say that plastic bags of Roller ground meal were lighted and let drop bit by bit over him till his skin peeled off from his knees to his hair, till his mind collapsed, peeled off, and he died of the pain in his own voice....

The soldiers focused on this one activity with force and intensity, their faces expressionless, . . ., as they slid into the shoulder high grass, the night empty of a single star. . . . they had already forgotten Mahlathini and the pillar of flame they had left behind. (131-134)

Yvonne Vera's novel gives actual place names and dates so that the locations are easily recognised in South Matabeleland and the violence is well documented.[6] However, there was a difference between the behaviour of the 5th Brigade in the North and the South. The frightening attacks in Matebeleland North in which single villages and individuals were subject to rape, murder, beatings and torture, were substituted in the Matebeleland South by prison camps where large numbers of people were imprisoned and beaten. The practical effect of Vera's transference of the tactics of violence from the North to the events in the South is to make this violence no longer a single, aberrant issue but a statement on the condition of Zimbabwe.

If all that Yvonne Vera had achieved was an account of the violence in Zimbabwe, then her story would scarcely differ from the reality which was often more shocking and cruel. But Vera goes a step further by seeking an explanation in the present with its power struggles and in the past with a history of violence. Additionally, she creates a space for the future in a process of reconciliation based on mutual humanity.

Yvonne Vera's main protagonist, Nonceba, finally finds peace beyond the traumatic experiences she has suffered. Her road to recovery begins at the hospital and in her home village and leads ultimately to an independent life in Bulawayo in the company of Cephas who, unknown to Nonceba, was Thenjiwe's lover just before independence. When Cephas reads about Thenjiwe's death and Nonceba's mutilation, he is in despair and visits Nonceba at the hospital. It is through Cephas that Nonceba finds her way back to life. He travels to Kezi and begs, insists and persuades Nonceba to leave the "naked graveyard" of Kezi and to accompany him to Bulawayo. In the meeting between Nonceba och Cephas, Vera describes the preconditions that will determine their lives in the future:

> Thenjiwe had been with this man, touched him. What had Thenjiwe loved about him? Was it his eyebrows like dark ink? His voice, gentle, forceful, confident? His kindness? His offer perhaps at all times to help, his capacity to surrender his life to others, herself, the sister? His spontaneous will? His ability to grasp another's pain? Was that it? *Nonceba looks into this stranger's eyes, searching in them for the distant place where love, not hurt, begins.* (160, my emphasis)

Here Vera depicts a different kind of male, not Sibaso, the deranged dissident or the cold-blooded soldiers of the 5th Brigade. This man is gentle, sensitive and thoughtful; he is a man in whom Nonceba can place her trust, and with whom she can deal with her trauma. It becomes a process of reconciliation with the past that lies on the personal level. Nonceba trusts Cephas and moves into his apartment in Bulawayo and they engage in a mutual processing of their sorrow with the absent Thenjiwe — Nonceba's much admired sister and the love of Cephas's life – continually present. In the end, they come to terms with their loss and find each other. Nonceba, above all, regains her self-confidence and one day she succeeds in finding a job all by herself.

Yvonne Vera exploits the fullness of language to describe violence in detail and to articulate the sensual responses in the lives of the victims. Above all, she demonstrates how reconciliation on a personal level, in which mutual respect and humanity are allowed to flourish, offers hope for the future.

Sindiwe Magona's novel *Mother to Mother*, (1998) is composed as a plea of understanding from the mother of a young black man who has killed a young white girl to the mother of the victim.[7] Amy Biehl, a young American scholar, was set upon by a crowd of young people and stabbed to death in Guguletu Township, Cape Town, South Africa, on 25th August 1993.[8] Four young men were arrested and tried for this crime. They were sentenced in October 1994. Their case was reviewed by the Truth and Reconciliation Commission (TRC) in 1997 within the terms of the remit that an "amnesty shall be granted in respect of acts, omissions and offences associated with political objectives committed in the course of the conflicts of the past," and the men were granted amnesty and released in 1998 (TRC 1997 and 1998).[9]

Magona's novel, published the same year as the TRC amnesty, contributes to the debate on the legitimacy of crowd action in the two descriptions of "the crowd" that frame this story. They mediate a perception of the crowd, both in general terms and in the particular circumstances of South Africa in the 1990s. Magona intimates that crowd violence is a non-reflective action arising from the heat of the moment and which, in the South African context, has its origins in a brutal, oppressive history. In her preface, Magona situates 'the crowd' for the reader by referring to it as "a mob of black youth" and to the killers as "lost creatures", which has a bearing on attitudes to the legal and moral responsibilities of those constituting the crowd. Magona's literary representation mediates the crowd, in terms of non-thinking, anonymous, group behaviour and, thereby, individually non-accountable.

The novel's two 'crowd scenes' have distinctly different articulations. Yet, in both cases, there are strong similarities to the essentialist and ahistorical analyses of crowds found in Elias Canetti's seminal work *Crowds and Power* (1962), in which categories of crowd violence are characterised in socio-psychological terms. The second scene, which is my focus here, describes the attack on Amy Biehl in a language that has uncanny similarities to Canetti's description of the baiting crowd (Canetti 48). Cannetti considers this to be the oldest form of a crowd and describes it as follows:

> The baiting crowd forms with reference to a quick attainable goal. The goal is known and clearly marked and is also near. The crowd is out for killing and knows what it wants to kill. It heads for the goal with unique determination and cannot be cheated of it. The proclaiming of the goal, the spreading about of who it is that it is to finish, is enough to make the crowd form. (Canetti 49)

Magona 'proclaims the goal' with the cry "One Settler, One Bullet", the PAC slogan which *"rings out* sending a shock-wave through the hoards all around this part of NY 1. Not yet a crowd. Nothing binds them yet" (205, my emphasis). The cry is *"repeated"* and *"re-echoed"* and "the same baptising cries meld the disparate individuals and little groups, isolated but a minute before, into a one-minded monster. A group. *A crowd, with one aim, one goal* . . ." (206, my emphasis).

Magona's development of crowd violence continues in the same vein as Canetti's characterisation: "This concentration on killing is of a special kind and of an unsurpassed intensity. Everyone wants to participate; everyone strikes a blow. . . . The speed, elation and conviction of a baiting crowd is something uncanny" (Canetti, 49). Magona's crowd follows the same pattern: "The pack races towards the source of the cry, as one echoing: 'One settler, one bullet'" (206). Her description generates intensity of action and the language of the narrator situates his/her perception of the crowd: "Mxolisi's crowd quickly disintegrates, each person going full speed to the epicentre . . ." (206), "the young men . . .have reached the *mob* . . .", the *"frenzied* cry", "the *milling* crowd" (207), the *"mob* of bodies" around the car (208, my emphasis). This is not a highly excited, mindless mass.

As Canneti argues, "the baiting crowd . . . goes back to the most primitive dynamic unit known among men: the hunting pack" (Canetti 50). Canetti is also at pains to point out that the "choice of the term pack . . . is intended to remind us that it owes its origin among men to the example of animals, the pack of animals hunting together. . . . men have learnt from wolves" (Canetti 96). When Amy Biehl and her friends leave the car and run to a service station for shelter, Magona's description, likewise, abandons human imagery to appropriate that of the hunt, the chase: "Smelling the climax, the *pack* is hot on their heels", "the *mob*, like *hounds*, give chase, yelling and screaming in glee" (208, my emphasis). Her use of a range of negative terms, including "pack", emphasises the primitiveness of crowd violence.

In the final act of the hunt, Magona reintroduces Mxolisi's mother as the narrative voice. The act of killing is carried out by "My son" cheered on by a "fervid" crowd crying "Amandla! Ngawethu! Power is ours!" and shouting the slogan "BOERS, THEY ARE DOGS" (209). Magona's narrative reaches the "irrevocable moment" when Mxolisi plunges his knife into Amy Biehl's body, fatally wounding her (209). In keeping with the previous descriptions of crowd action, the lack of agency on the part of the attacker is reinforced in his mother's appeal: "My son was only an agent, executing the long-simmering dark desires of his race" (210).

Magona seems to be concerned to demonstrate that there is no individual culpability in this act, rather that there is a collective responsibility derived from a history of oppression of the apartheid system. She also adheres to a perception of crowd behaviour as a regression to primitive forms of existence rather than the individualised, rational, group-identity process that is characteristic of modern historical and psycho-sociological narratives.

In her preface, Magona explains her choice of perspective—of the murderer and his family—by asking if "there are no lessons to be had from knowing something of the other world [...] of those [...] whose environment failed to nurture them in the higher ideals of humanity and who, instead, became lost creatures of malice and destruction". The environment of which she speaks is "the legacy of apartheid—a system repressive and brutal, that bred senseless inter- and intra-racial violence".

But Magona also sees, in the act of writing itself, a form of reconciliation as the novel is intended to communicate across the gap of loss and understanding in the hope that it might "ease the other mother's pain . . . if a little."

In their different ways the three writers discussed here exploit the imaginative qualities of language to explore the effects of violence on individuals and societies. More importantly, they also use the creative space afforded by the narrative form of the novel to find ways in which individuals can find solace in human interaction, human trust and human kindness. Central to the work of all three writers is recognition that the creative process—the act of writing—is, in itself, an important constituent of the process of transformation in the perceptions and insights of individuals and societies if the horrors of the past are to be avoided.

References

Austen, Benjamin (2005), An interview with Zakes Mda. nat creole.magazine. arts. culture. life. Online. http://www.natcreole.com/features.htm#title1 Part i accessed 16th Dec 2005. Part ii accessed 19th Jan. 2006.

Bell, David. n.d. "'Sätt att dö; sätt att leva': våld och litteratur i Sydafrika och Zimbabwe." In Carita Bäckström and Mai Palmberg eds. *Kul-tur i Afrika*. Uppsala: NAI, forthcoming.

Bornman, Elirea, René van Eeden and Marie Wentzel (eds) (1998), *Violence in South Africa: A Variety of Perspectives*. Pretoria: Human Sciences Research Council.

Canetti, Elias (1962), *Crowds and Power*. Trans Carol Stewart. London: Victor Gollancz.

CCJPZ. (1999), *Breaking the silence, Building True Peace: a report into the disturbances in Matabeleland and the Midlands, 1980-1988*. Np: Catholic Commission for Justice and Peace in Zimbabwe. Legal Resources Foundation.

Croft, Andy (1990), *Red Letter Days*. London: Lawrence and Wishart. (1998),. *A Weapon in the Struggle*. London: Pluto.

Ernst Ulrike (2002), *From Anti-Apartheid to African Renaissance*. Hamburg: LIT.

Holloway, Myles (1988), An interview with Zakes Mda (Feb. 7, 1987). *South Africa Theatre Journal* Vol 2 No. 2. 81-88.

Kearney, J. A(2003), *Representing Dissension. Riot, Rebellion and Resistance in the South African English Novel*. Pretoria: University of South Africa Press.

Magona, Sindiwe (1999), *Mother to Mother*. Claremont SA: David Philip 1998; Boston USA: Beacon Books.

Magubane, Peter (1986), Soweto: *The Fruit of Fear*. Foreword by Desmond Tutu. Grand Rapids Mich: Eerdmans; Trenton NJ: Africa World Press.

Mashabela, Harry (1986), *Black South Africa. A People on the Boil (1976-1986)*. Excerpt in Magubane.

Mda, Zakes (1995), *Ways of Dying*. Cape Town: OUP.

Minnaar Anthony, Sam Pretorius and Marie Wentzel (1998), "Political conflict and other manifestations of violence in South Africa." In Bornman *et al* 1998.

Muponde, Robert and Mandi Taruvinga (eds) (2003), *Sign and Taboo: Perspectives on the poetic fiction of Yvonne Vera*. Harare: Weaver Press, 2002; Oxford: James Curry.

Oakes, Dougie, ed (1994), *Reader's Digest Illustrated History of South Africa*. 3rd Edition. Cape Town: Reader's Digest.

TRC (1997), Truth and Reconciliation Commission Amnesty Hearings, Cape Town: 8 July 1997.

TRC (1998), Truth and Reconciliation Amnesty, Cape Town: 28th July 1998.

Vera, Yvonne. (2002), *The Stone Virgins*. New York: Farrar, Straus and Giroux; Zimbabwe: Weaver Press.

ZHRA (1999), *Choosing the Path to Peace and Development. Coming to Terms with Human Rights Violations of the 1982-1987 Conflict in Matabeleland and Midlands Provinces*. Harare: Zimbabwe Human Rights Association.

Notes

[1] For an overview of this debate in South Africa see Ulrike Ernst, *From Anti-Apartheid to African Renaissance*, (Hamburg: LIT, 2002).

[2] This is also a matter of some contemporary concern as the case of the suspended production of Mozart's "Idomeneo" by the Deutsche Opera in Berlin illustrates. In a wider geographical context reference can be made to Britain in the first half of the 20th century where during the First World War the War Propaganda Bureau enlisted famous writers to produce fictional works depicting the barbarity of the enemy. In other words to create a fiendish Other. John Buchan with his spy novels *Greenmantle* and *The Thirty Nine Steps*, was one of these (See National Archives UK). The reverse side of this process was the literary "flowering" of working-class and proletarian fiction in the 1920s and 1930s. Though intended as a revolutionary literature its literary and critical development was hampered by the critical demands of the British Communist Party and their allies who were greatly influenced by the USSR and the demands for socialist-realist writing rather than imaginative and creative fiction. (See Andy Croft *Red Letter Days* [London: Lawrence and Wishart, 1990] and *A Weapon in the Struggle* [London: Pluto, 1998]; and David Bell, *Ardent Propaganda* [Umeå: Umeå University, 1995])

[3] The sections on Zakes Mda and Yvonne Vera are based on my article "'Sätt att dö; sätt att leva': våld och litteratur i Sydafrika och Zimbabwe" in Carita Bäckström and Mai Palmberg eds *Kul-tur i Afrika* (Uppsala: NAI forthcoming). The Yvonne Vera section is also indebted to my contribution to "Yvonne Vera and Women's Writing in Zimbabwe: A Symposium", at the Blekinge Institute of

Technology, Department of English, Karlskrona, Sweden. 2 December 2005, titled "Yvonne Vera in Harmony and Discord: Postcolonial Poetics in *Butterfly Burning* (1998) and Post Colonial Violence in *The Stone Virgins* (2002)". The section on Sindiwe Magona is based on my paper "Collective Responsibility and Individual Culpability in Sindiwe Magona's *Mother to Mother*" presented at the "Riots in Literature" Seminar at the ESSE 8 Conference, London 2006.

4   For a study of the violence in South Africa in this period see Elirea Bornman, René van Eeden och Marie Wentzel (eds), *Violence in South Africa: A Variety of Perspectives* (Pretoria: Human Sciences Research Council, 1998)

5   For a full discussion of Yvonne Vera's work see Robert Muponde and Mandi Taruvinga, (eds), *Sign and Taboo: Perspectives on the Poetic Fiction of Yvonne Vera* (Harare: Weaver Press, 2002; Oxford: James Curry, 2003).

6   See the Catholic Commission for Justice and Peace in Zimbabwe (CCJPZ) in a report from 1997 and the short version in 1999: *Breaking the Silence, Building True Peace: a report into the disturbances in Matabeleland and the Midlands 1980-1988* (np: Catholic Commission for Justice and Peace in Zimbabwe. Legal Resources Foundation, 1999). See also the Zimbabwe Human Rights Association's (ZHRA) documentation 1999: *Choosing the Path to Peace and Development. Coming to Terms with Human Rights Violations of the 1982-1987 Conflict in Matabeleland and Midlands Provinces.*(Harare: Zimbabwe Human Rights Association, 1999)

7   It should be noted that Sindiwe Magona's novel is not the first to deal in detail with township unrest and the murder of a white person. Harry Bloom's *Transvaal Episode* (1956) is based loosely on the defiance campaigns of 1952. (See Kearney 246-268)

8   This was not the only case of violence or one involving the death of a white person. It happened in Port Elizabeth in 1952, in Sharpeville 1960, in Soweto 1976 and in the disturbances in the townships during the State of Emergency in 1985. (See *Reader's Digest* and Magubane) In 1993 4,398 people died in political/unrest violence, 562 of them in the month of August alone (see Minaar et al 19). 1993 was particularly violent: Chris Hani the leader of the ANC armed wing was murdered in April, bloody conflicts were the pattern for the political rivalries of

the ANC and the Inkatha Freedom Party, the PAC persisted in a continuation of the battle on the streets and white death squads were believed by many to be active throughout the country. (See *Reader's Digest* 494-511 and Minaar et al.13-19)

9   The TRC was set up under the Promotion of National Unity and Reconciliation Act, 1995

Chapter 14

"I CAN SPEAK IF I WANT TO SPEAK ... WOULD YOU HEAR ME IF I CALLED?" THE POLITICS OF REPRESENTATION AND THE POETICS OF RECEPTION IN *WHAT IS THE WHAT: THE AUTOBIOGRAPHY OF VALENTINO ACHAK DENG*

John Masterson

"There are none so ignorant of geography as those with their military bases in every quarter of the planet. It is possible to have satellites which survey every square inch of the globe while producing schoolchildren who think Malawi is a Disney character."
(Terry Eagleton – *Holy Terror*)[1]

"It is criminal that all of this has happened, and has been allowed to happen.
In a furious blast, I kick and kick again, flailing my body like a fish run aground. Hear me, Christian neighbors! Hear your brother just above! Nothing again. No one is listening. No one is waiting to hear the kicking of a man above. It is unexpected. You have no ears for someone like me."
(Dave Eggers – *What is the What*)[2]

"Do the people in America really want to read this?"
(Odette Nyiramilimo)[3]

At the margins of *Orientalism*, Edward Said includes the following epigraph from Marx's *The Eighteenth Brumaire of Louis Bonaparte*: "They cannot represent themselves; they must be represented."[4] In June 2008, five years after Said's death and thirty years after the original publication of his seminal study, an exhibition, entitled 'The Lure of the East: British Orientalist Painting,' opened at the Tate Britain.[5] For twenty-first century visitors, the show's focus on the eighteenth and nineteenth centuries of high imperial expansion seemed to have peculiar resonance, both culturally and politically. For those inclined and/or able to think back to the jingoistic declaration of the 'War on Terror,' certain haunting continuities seemed to exist between strategies used then and now. Intense debates surrounding Said's legacy continue today. Concerns with the politics and poetics of representing and/or misrepresenting other peoples, cultures and histories pervade both seminar and newsrooms. In these times of global credit crunchery, the spectres of Marx seem to be with us in more ways than one.

Such broad questions inform the following analysis of *What is the What*. Dave Eggers' text is based on the testimony of Valentino Achak Deng, a Sudanese 'Lost Boy' who was scheduled to fly into America on the very day other planes flew into the Twin Towers.[6] Eventually airlifted from a Kenyan refugee camp, he was relocated to the States where he currently lives. Widely regarded as one of the hot young things of American letters, Eggers achieved notoriety and recognition for his debut novel, *A Heartbreaking Work of Staggering Genius*.[7] Published in 2000 and classified as a 'memoir,' the text draws from his experience of losing both parents within weeks of each other. Whilst Eggers' literary experimentalism is at times indulgent, the book comes close to living up to its ironically inflated title.

What is the What constitutes a certain mutation and maturation of this factual/fictional approach. For Erik Henriksen, the novel signals an "eschewing [of Eggers'] usual self-centeredness and postmodern playfulness."[8] To a large extent, this is the result of the apparently radically different subject matter and subject himself. This 'apparently' is significant, as some critics suggest Egger's debut is his own account of being a 'lost boy.' Whilst signposting such possible links may have value, attentive readers will be wary of conflating distinct experiences by applying umbrella labels. The contrasts are equally as important, if not more so, than the comparisons. Rather than attempt to re-create the introspective intensity of *A Heartbreaking Work*, Eggers accepts the alternative challenge of turning his gaze outwards to help tell another's story.

Whilst this collection is concerned with African authors and conflicts, I propose some of the issues raised by *What is the What* correspond to associated debates about how writers represent the unrepresentable; in this case, the protracted Sudanese Civil War and its fallout. I argue that, in both textual and contextual terms, this novel is concerned with the political process of telling stories and the willingness, or otherwise, of various audiences to listen. Questions concerning power relations between American writer and African informant remain central. Ultimately, however, *What is the What* is an engaging work that challenges limiting perceptions by promoting the values of genuinely humanistic exchange.

Produced and consumed in an age of e-books, the novel is aimed at a Western, predominantly American readership. For those uninitiated in the complexities of Sudanese socio and geo-political history, yet with access to cyberspace, an informative guide is provided via the Valentino Achak Deng Foundation website.[9] Compiled by Greg Larsen, it includes tips for lobbying U.S. Congress members on the 'Sudanese Question,' alongside a selective chronology of events pertinent to the book. It also features a revealing interview with Deng and Eggers. This clearly explains the genesis and development of their project:

> Eggers: 'The first thing we did was just get through the basic story ... I spent some time transcribing and reviewing [it] ... At that point, we really hadn't decided whether I was just helping Valentino write his own book, or if I was writing a book about him.'
>
> Deng: 'I thought I might want to write my own book, but I learned that I was not ready to do this. I was still taking classes in basic writing at Georgia Perimeter College.'
>
> Eggers: 'I really didn't know exactly what form it would finally take — whether it would be first person or third, whether it would be fiction or nonfiction. After about 18 months of struggle with it, we settled on a fictionalized autobiography, in Valentino's voice ... All of the events in the book have historical basis. But it really is a novel. I made up many scenes that were necessary to describe the whole sweep of those twenty or so years that the book covers. Sometimes I'd read a human rights report about a certain incident during the civil war, and would ask Val if he knew someone who had experienced that incident, or something like it. Sometimes he did know someone, and we could go from there, but other times I had to imagine it on my own. Some of these scenes were necessary to include, even if Val didn't have personal experience with them.'

Whilst there are significant references to the practical obstacles they had to overcome, perhaps the most striking term is 'struggle.' The project's conception, as well as its conceptual phase, was marked with certain uncertainty; neither participant seeming sure what the result might be. The book's gestation period was similarly protracted, with its birth proving no less problematic.

An alternative interpretation of this struggle would attend to questions of voice and genre. More than a convenient way of side-stepping the issue of textual definition, Eggers' categorisation of *What is the What* as a "fictionalized autobiography in Valentino's voice" is accurate and enabling. The novelist is given and oftentimes revels in a certain latitude when it comes to dealing with historical matters. Yet it is the way Eggers manipulates and amplifies this voice that opens up avenues into, rather than away from, a host of complex and compelling questions about geo-political turbulence within Sudan and, critically, its global mediation and reception. This corresponds with the symbiotic, or otherwise, nature of various relationships (Deng/Eggers, Novel/Critique, Africa/America) so fundamental to this text.

For Graham Huggan, 'paratextual' features ("jacket blurbs and designs, editorial comments and notes, glossaries etc.") have central rather than peripheral significance for various novels.[10] In the dog-eat-dog world of literary sales, promotion by association is equally prized. As such, Khaled Hosseini's tribute on the front cover of *What is the What* is crucial: "told with humour, humanity, and bottomless compassion for his subject...It is impossible to read this book and not be humbled, enlightened, transformed." This is high praise from the author of *The Kite Runner*, set in Taliban-era Afghanistan and recently made into a film. The implication behind this commendation, sanctioned by Eggers' New York publishers, might be that, like Hosseini, his writing has the humanistic (because creative) capacity to illuminate previously 'dark' areas of the world. *What is the What* is promoted as and, to a certain extent, succeeds in being a transformative supplement to the twenty second news-clips on 'regional instability' with which CNN and other major news providers routinely package up and pedal reports on Africa to their American consumers. Again and again, such debates refer us back to Said's preoccupation with the discursive construction, representation and control exerted over 'other' cultures and spaces. This becomes a critical textual as well as contextual preoccupation for Eggers and Deng.

What is the What is 'contrapuntally' arranged, with alternate chapters dealing with Deng's trials and tribulations as an alien in America.[11] These are interspersed with sprawling sections dedicated to his displacement from Sudan during the civil war of the early 1980s and his resultant epic journeys through refugee camps from Kenya to Ethiopia. Various critics have suggested the novel's success owes much to its ability to maintain this balance between Deng's Diasporic experiences both in Africa and America. Such qualitative judgments raise a host of questions, perhaps none more so than that of target audience. This, in turn, corresponds with some of the novel's didactic and/or corrective aims.

At various points, Deng confronts a homogenising geo-political ignorance from certain American hosts. The trenchant implication is that this is symptomatic of a wider geo-political arrogance linked to the U.S.'s global authority, perceived or otherwise. Told in Deng's imagined first-person, the voice maintained throughout, the following, early episode concerns the ransacking of his Atlanta apartment. Physical and verbal abuse aside, it is the hopelessly wayward geographical reference that appears most significant:

> 'He kicks me in the stomach, and now the shoulder ... "Fucking Nigerian motherfucker!" ... "No wonder you motherfuckers are in the Stone Age!" He gives me one more kick, lighter than the others, but this one directly into my temple, and a burst of white light fills my left eye. In America I have been called Nigerian before – it must be the most familiar of African countries – but I have never been kicked. Again, though, I have seen it happen. I suppose there is little in the way of violence that I have not seen in Sudan, in Kenya. I spent years in a refugee camp in Ethiopia, and there I watched two young boys, perhaps twelve years old, fighting so viciously over rations that one kicked the other one to death.'[12]

Expletives apart, this excerpt appears indicative of the approach taken in and the power of the narrative more widely. As a reader, we shift from Atlanta apartment to Ethiopian refugee camp in the space of sentences. The bloody thread connecting American city and African camp is violence. Here, Deng's fictionally-mediated voice assures us that he has borne witness. Phrases such as "I have seen it happen" and "I was there" pepper the narrative, lending it coherence and seemingly authenticating his truly fantastic, intermittently horrific testimonial. In terms of a skewed political-geography lesson, however, it is the conflation of the African continent with one of its most recognisable, if internally disparate and dynamic, nation-states that remains most striking. The reader cannot help but imagine Eggers' head hanging under the shameful burden of his countrymen's ignorance. One of the most striking ironies of this earliest encounter is that Deng is beaten, robbed and wrongly called Nigerian by African-Americans. It seems the bonds of racial solidarity are not strong enough to insure more attentive map-readings.

Such textual episodes relate to another of *What is the What*'s key paratextual features. Before encountering Deng's 2007 preface, we are presented with a regional map, comprising Sudan, the North Western tip of Kenya and the Western half of Ethiopia. It provides the reader with some sense of geographical relativity and immensity, offering a re-orienting reference during sections when Eggers recreates Deng's journey. As Francine Prose suggests, "[by] the time the members of Eggers's large and youthful fan base have repeatedly consulted the book's map of East Africa, tracing the Lost Boys' wanderings, they will be able to visualize the geographical positions of Sudan, Ethiopia and Kenya with a clarity surpassing their possibly hazy recall of anything they might have memorized for a World Civilization class."[13] The map thus complements numerous instances where author and informant strive to illuminate some of Sudan's socio-political dimensions, both temporally and spatially. Rather than bludgeon us with chronologies of dates and events, Deng and Eggers connect the history to, by bringing it alive through, the former's story. In terms of encouraging the reader to come to a more qualified, because complicating, appreciation of the entangled issues and challenges facing a country the size of Western Europe, the choice to fictionalise the testimonial raw material may not be as misguided as some critics have suggested.[14]

The map's political function chimes with the overarching objective of challenging the notion that Sudanese politics can be conflated with events in Darfur. *What is the What* is at pains to emphasise the colonially-intertwined narratives and tensions of the country's Northern and Southern halves. Crucially, their differences from the specificities of Darfur, both then and now, are foregrounded. Time and again, this is allegorically realised through Deng's struggle to have his story heard and grasped by various American hosts. One such incident involves a policewoman investigating the robbery. Swept away on the stream of Deng's internal monologue, the reader's geo-politics lesson is announced with, '[it] is a fact that Darfur is now better known than the country in which that region sits.' Whilst this may seem a little heavy-handed, it is lent humanising delicacy by Deng and Achor Achor's voices and faces:

'We explain the geography briefly.

"Sudan, wow," she says, halfheartedly inspecting the locks on our front door. "What are you doing here?"

We tell her that we're working and trying to go to college.

"So were you part of the genocide? Victims of that?"

I sit down, and Achor Achor tries to clarify things for her ... Achor Achor explains where we came from, and our relationship with the Darfurians, and it's only when he mentions that some from that region have come to Atlanta to live that she seems interested ... We greeted [the Darfurians] then and after Church, surprised to see them among us, and curious to know what they had planned. It was not customary for Darfurians, most of whom were Muslim, to be mixing with Dinka, and unprecedented for them to be attending a Christian church on a Sunday. The Darfurians historically had identified more with the Arabs than with us, even though they resembled us far more closely than the ethnic Arabs. Our feelings about them had long been complicated, too, by the fact that many of the murahaleen raiders who terrorized our villages were from Darfur; it took us some time to know that those who were suffering in this new stage of the civil war were not our oppressors, but were victims like ourselves. And so we let them be, and they us. But all is different now, and alliances are changing.'[15]

Whilst there is a latent critique of her ignorance, it is sensitively, perhaps even sympathetically, rendered. Final allusions to these ever-fluid diaspora networks prompt further reflections on the dynamics and potentially enabling exchanges between various insiders and outsiders (Sudanese/American, Achor Achor/Policewoman, Reader/Text, Deng/Eggers). By offering a more qualified insight into these provisional groups and their negotiations, both within and beyond Sudan, the passage cautions us not to judge the policewoman too harshly. With this caveat in mind, such episodes function as variations on a central textual aim; to encourage us, as members of supposedly international communities, readerly and political, to listen a little more carefully to those other voices and stories behind the headlines. As such, the policewoman's allusion to 'genocide' offers a provocative connection with another American writer concerned with African conflict.

In 2000, Philip Gourevitch published his account of the aftermath of the Rwandan genocide. *We Wish to Inform You That Tomorrow We Will be Killed with Our Families: Stories from Rwanda* has been described as essential reading for anyone involved in international humanitarian work. As my final epigraph suggests, Gourevitch's book, like Eggers', was aimed at a predominantly Western audience. Like Eggers, it was in large part designed to prompt an American readership to challenge inherited caricatures about innate African political 'primitivism,' which seemingly spawned never-ending cycles of violence. Key sections of *We Wish to Inform You* explore the legacy of Belgian colonial rule and the decisively divisive hand it played in manipulating ethnic differences between Hutu and Tutsi communities. Like Eggers, Gourevitch includes various maps which become essential rather than extraneous to the critical thinking experience.

As someone aiming to disturb the 'Heart of Darkness' rhetoric surrounding Rwanda, Gourevitch's commendation of Eggers' book warrants forensic analysis: "*What is the What* is a novel that possesses the best qualities of a documentary film: the conviction of truthfulness, and the constant reminder of the arbitrariness of fate, for worse and for better. By setting his story of African annihilation and survival as a story of American immigration, Eggers ensures that it belongs to us all, as it must."[16] There are several revealing aspects to this description. The notion that the text has a cinematic sweep supports analyses of its contrapuntal plot and pace. Both African and American journeys are thematically and structurally intertwined. For the sensitive reader, this can have a marked impact. As we read, we experience these entangled plotlines, times and spaces on the page. Translated at a broader geo-political level, this captures one of Eggers' and Gourevitch's major preoccupations; namely, that events, whether taking place in a remote Rwandan village or a Kenyan I.D.P. camp, are never quite as distinct and/or otherworldly as they at first appear. As this fictionalised account of Deng's story suggests, lives and narratives, both individual and collective, are always already much more knotted. By devoting sections of their works to the legacies of British and Belgian colonial powers in Sudan and Rwanda respectively, as well as the influence of various international administrations in humanitarian or other guises, both Eggers and Gourevitch suggest that forging and exposing such links has always and will remain politically vital.

Yet it is Gourevitch's definition of the text as Eggers' story of African annihilation and tenuous State-side survival that allows us to broach the biggest, arguably most problematic issue of all. Whose story is *What is the What*? Gourevitch refers to the necessity of 'us' taking narrative ownership, but who does this 'us' include? Do such acts of appropriation involve the dispossession and/or deprivation of others? Does the act of 'taking ownership' constitute an alternative form of colonisation (narrative or otherwise)? Or, is it rather more concerned with revealing the entwined nature of all such stories in the hope that their burdens of significance might be better shared in future?[17]

Such questions inevitably overlap with issues of representation, voice and agency alluded to in my introduction. They may also chime with debates central to, yet never quite settled, in Gayatri Spivak's provocative discussion of subaltern speech and practice.[18] I suggest *What is the What* demands and deserves similarly flexible approaches. Rather than viewing the fact that it poses more questions than it provides answers as a weakness, it might be reassessed as an intriguing possibility and strength. In this salvaging rather than savaging spirit, attention to a term that recurs in different reviews may prove helpful. It also facilitates a return to the text.

For both *The Sunday Herald* (Scotland) and *The Observer* (England), the most fitting description of the Eggers/Deng double-act is 'ventriloquism.' For Kevin MacNeil, *What is the What* is "a stunning act of symbiotic literary ventriloquism, [in which] Eggers and Deng have evinced that nightmarish world of Sudanese civil war which so many endured and so few survived. It's ultimately a work of deep psychological trauma and impossible, marvellous triumph."[19] For Tim Adams, the novel is "an emotional primer about the impacted recent history of the Sudan, about the fighting between north and south, government and rebels, Arabs and Dinka, murahaleen and SPLA, [and as such] Eggers' ventriloquism could hardly be bettered. He makes Achak's an authentic and affecting voice of the grimmest narrative of our times."[20] When compared with Gourevitch's description, it is notable that Deng merits a mention. Here, *What is the What* is seen as a genuinely collaborative effort, embarked upon and delivered for the ultimate benefit of a much wider reading public. Accordingly, 'symbiosis' and 'voice' remain keywords. Yet, the prominence of 'ventriloquism' becomes most revealing when considering the power relationships between Eggers as alien writer and Deng as native informant.

A return to the preface might clarify some of these issues. Admitting his writerly limitations, Deng talks of relaying the testimonial raw material from which Eggers fashioned a "work of art." For those concerned with the veracity of the resulting narrative, he adds a familiar disclaimer:

> 'It should be known to the readers that I was very young when some of the events in the book took place, and as a result we simply had to pronounce *What is the What* a novel. I could not, for example, recount some conversations that took place seventeen years ago. However it should be noted that all of the major events in the book are true. The book is historically accurate, and the world I have known is not different from the one depicted in these pages. We live in a time where even the most horrific events in this book could occur, and in most cases, did occur. For example, between May 16, 1983 and January 9, 2005 over two and a half million people died of war and war-related causes in Sudan, over four million people were internally displaced in southern Sudan and nearly two million southern Sudanese took refuge in foreign countries.'[21]

Concerned with humanitarian crimes that assume a macabre reality beyond the imagination of the most twisted horror writer, this is an alternative *Heartbreaking Work*. Its various commitments exorcise the ghost of postmodern solipsism. If questions remain about the internal dynamics of the Deng/Eggers collaboration, it is essential to acknowledge another symbiotic relationship alluded to in the preface and returned to throughout the book.

Deng is blissfully clear when outlining the imperatives behind the project: "I wanted to reach out to others to help them understand Sudan's place in our global community. I am relieved that Dave and I have accomplished this task through illumination of my life as an example of atrocities many successive governments of Sudan committed against its own people."[22] Several key concerns are signposted here. There is the familiar didactic element; Deng is clearly appealing to a Western audience and, in conjunction with Eggers, he is driven by the desire to challenge received stereotypes about African civil conflicts. The essential method for disturbing, if not totally disavowing them, is to appeal to a shared humanity with an unknown reader by recounting his own experiences. Whilst familiarity can often breed contempt, the strategy of foregrounding the micro as a way of reflecting the macro remains an effective one. It also corresponds with another central preoccupation.

At various points, Deng reflects on the need to tell his unique story in honour of compatriots who died on the road, never completing the journey to tell their own. The novel is galvanised by such multiple motivations. The personal and political, individual and collective desires to communicate various stories are inextricably bound together. The reader's qualitative judgment of the book will have much to do with how effectively and, perhaps, ethically they feel this marriage is sustained. On all its various levels, therefore, *What is the What* serves as an extensive and intensive meditation on the need for certain voices and stories to be heard. As Deng himself states towards the close of his preface, "I am blessed to have lived to inform you that even when my hours were darkest, I believed that someday I could share my experiences with others. This book is a form of struggle, and it keeps my faith alive to struggle."[23] It is revealing that both American writer and African informant use 'struggle' to describe the simultaneous pains and pleasures that marked the text's conception, development and delivery. Certain questions, however, remain for its recipient readers.

When attempting to render the traumas of war and dispossession, *What is the What* morphs into a struggle for the reader. Littered with bodies of the dead and dying, it does, at times, resemble an apocalyptic documentary. Yet, for strategic, humanistic reasons, this seems precisely the point. In this regard, Eggers' reference to reading and incorporating material from Human Rights reports assumes greater significance. If a fictional text is to effectively engage with such palpable suffering, it cannot result in a passive, indifferent reading experience. Thus, if you judge the book a success, the real symbiotic relationship exceeds the author/informant dualism. The true connections must be forged between Deng, Eggers and us as readers. Deng's preface concludes with a unifying flourish: "Since you and I exist, together we can make a difference!"[24] It is only once we reach the novel's end that we appreciate this is much more than a utopian and/or Geldofian gesture:

> 'It gives me strength, almost unbelievable strength, to know that you are there. I covet your eyes, your ears, the collapsible space between us. How blessed are we to have each other? I am alive and you are alive so we must fill the air with our words ... I will tell stories to people who will listen and to people who don't want to listen, to people who seek me out and to those who run. All the while I will know that you are there. How can I pretend that you do not exist? It would be almost as impossible as you pretending that I do not exist.'[25]

An attentive reading of this passage proves typically rewarding.

Both first and second person pronouns seem slippery, if not interchangeable, leading to the inevitable question, 'who is really talking and to whom?' Initially, it appears Deng is addressing us as his reader. He could just as feasibly, however, be addressing Eggers. Alternatively, it could be Eggers speaking to Deng. Is this the 'real' Deng or Eggers' fictional creation? Where does one end and the other begin? Whilst these questions assail the reader here as they do throughout, I suggest they do not significantly compromise the closing impression of and motivation for the book as a whole. The idea of 'collapsible space,' therefore, becomes the most significant because conceptually resonant.

Taken from different parts of *What is the What*, the title of this chapter indicates why this is a rich text to consider alongside other representations of African conflicts. From the novel's preface to its closing lines, both Eggers and Deng place the utmost importance on conveying this kaleidoscopic story. Painful and painstaking as the process may be, this voice projection encourages the reader to engage with the narrative as a means of exploring much wider sociological questions. Exploration of certain textual episodes will add flesh to these contextual bones.

On arrival in the United States, numerous Lost Boys were helped by various groups. In Deng's case, these included Atlanta-based Christian organisations. Rejoining him in the aftermath of the robbery, the reader discovers a man alone with his mouth gagged. The interior monologue details his struggles to alert his neighbours: "Soon I will be able to moisten the tape enough that my lips will be free ... I must make myself heard, I must alert a neighbor, bring someone to my door ... This ordeal needs to end."[26] It is the way Eggers uses such instances to dramatise and symbolise debates about speaking and listening, writing and reading that becomes compelling when considering matters of ventriloquism and representation. To a large extent, the narrative is held together by the narrator's repeated reflections on the painful necessity of communicating his story, both to an immediate audience, real or imagined, and a wider reading public. When compared with other descriptions of the trials and tribulations he endured during his central African exodus, there are striking parallels between Deng's demands in both settings.

In this instance, the metaphor is obvious. With his mouth literally and figuratively gagged, Deng's only means of communication is to bang through floors: "Christian neighbours below, where are you tonight? Are you home? Would you hear me if I called? ... Will you hear me kicking?"[27] Whilst such inserts might appear over-determined, I suggest Eggers and Deng use them in consistent, fairly subtle ways throughout. It is critical, for example, that notions of Christian fraternity and neighbourliness are gently satirised. In this instance, we are invited to dig a little deeper beneath the seemingly benevolent guise of the various groups taking an interest in the Lost Boys. No mere workaday Church-goers, some of Deng's most proactive neighbours are Evangelical Christians, bent on converting him and other immigrants, such as his Costa Rican neighbour, Edgardo. When we start digging, such religious recruitment drives seem eerily akin to those of neo-imperial missionaries. This corresponds with another micrologically and macrologically resonant issue in *What is the What*; the demand for and supply of various narratives.

Foregrounded early on, it is characteristically relevant both to the Eggers/Deng, writer/informant relationship and those involving various other narrative producers and consumers. Typically, one instance speaks volumes. Lying prostrate following the assault, Deng reflects on the suspicion and envy that has overwhelmed some of his fellow Sudanese in the Diaspora:

'Didn't we all walk across the desert? they ask. Didn't we all eat the hides of hyenas and goats to keep our bellies full? Didn't we all drink our own urine? This last part, of course, is apocryphal; absolutely not true for the majority of us, but it impresses people ... the tales of the Lost Boys have become remarkably similar over the years. Everyone's account includes attacks by lions, hyenas, crocodiles. All have borne witness to attacks by the murahaleen – government-sponsored militias on horseback – to Antonov bombings, to slave-raiding. But we did not all see the same things. At the height of our journey from southern Sudan to Ethiopia, there were perhaps twenty thousand of us, and our routes were very different. Some arrived with their parents. Others with rebel soldiers. A few thousand travelled alone. But now, sponsors and newspaper reporters and the like expect stories to have certain elements, and the Lost Boys have been consistent in their willingness to oblige. Survivors tell the stories the sympathetic want, and that means making them as shocking as possible. My own story includes enough small embellishments that I cannot criticize the accounts of others.[28]

Once again, the design and development of this passage is multiply revealing.

What begins as an apparent critique of internecine tensions within the ex-pat community, morphs into a much more sophisticated analysis of the relationship between host society and alien informants. In those overcrowded marketplaces populated by charitable organisations and news providers alike, the more sensationalist a story's ingredients ("if it bleeds, it leads"), the more likely it is to capture consumers' imaginations.[29] The trenchant suggestion is that this system of narrative demand and supply has resulted in the production of certain generic archetypes, exotically infused with the tails and tales of lions, hyenas and crocodiles. Whilst placing debates concerning the politics and economics of such testimonial narratives in a much broader, contested context, its final sentence also raises fundamental questions about the relationship between Deng's testimonial base and *What is the What's* novelistic superstructure. Such moments of self-reflexivity, where Deng and Eggers display, rather than attempt to conceal, their awareness of such marketplaces and forces, constitute some of the most compelling features of their text. By actively promoting rather than relegating these critical debates, the book attains that singularity which sets it apart from the formulaic.

Another memorable description, embedded in African soil, might also be used to support this point.

John Masterson

> 'When we left Ethiopia, so many died along the way. There were thousands of us together, but there were so many injured, so much blood along the path. This is when I saw more dead than at any other time. Women, children. Babies the size of the Quiet Baby who would not survive. There seemed to be no point. I look back on that year and see only disconnected and miscolored images, as in a fitful dream. I know that we were at Pochalla, then nearby, at Golkur, three hours away. It rained there with a constant grey fury for three months. At Golkur there were again SPLA soldiers and NGOs and food and, eventually, school. There we heard of the rebel split, when a Nuer commander named Riek Machar decided to leave and create his own rebel movement, the SPLA-Nasir, a group that would for some time cause the SPLA as much trouble as Khartoum. This resulting war within the war had Garang's Dinka rebels fighting Machar's Nuer rebels. So many tens of thousands were lost this way, and the infighting, the brutality involved, allowed the world to turn an indifferent eye to the decimation of Sudan: the civil war became, to the world at large, too confusing to decipher, a mess of tribal conflicts with no clear heroes and villains.'[30]

From the opening to the closing lines of this passage, the reader is struck by the scale of human suffering. Whilst the mind often balks at statistics of dead or dying, references to thousands and the blood-soaked women and children sacrificed to the road retain their gut-rending power. Yet, again, out of this seemingly anonymous mass emerges specific details, both personal and geographic. This conveys the critical impression, as it does throughout, that this particular story-teller was one of that mass, emerging to tell his tale in tribute to others less fortunate. At such instances, rather than pulling Deng's strings as puppet-master, Eggers' presence recedes into the background. Ultimately, it is the haunting composition of this freeze-frame, rather than quibbles about the composer, that captures our readerly attention.

The phrase 'I look back on that year' also foregrounds the retrospective nature of Deng's testimonial. This in turn reminds us of his preface reflections concerning the certain uncertainty of memory and his struggles (that keyword again) to retrieve the elusive details of previous experiences.[31] The passage thus captures the sense that *What is the What* is as concerned with Deng's temporal journeys as it is with his spatial ones. Specific place names are given, inviting us to refer back to the opening map. A sense of the text's organic unity and the critical role played by its paratextual features is once more conveyed. Coupled with this, we are given the identities of prominent political players, drawing our attention to the intense nature of various factional disputes and fallouts. If our heads spin under the joint pressures of thousands of corpses and dizzying allusions to warring factions, I maintain this is the very effect Deng/Eggers intend and that they in turn wish to interrogate.

Arguably, therefore, the passage's most critical term, and the one that provides a link between the specific textual and wider contextual concerns of *What is the What*, is 'decipher.' This can be interpreted as referring to how we all go about 'reading' ourselves, each other and the wider world. Essentially, it revolves around the connections between individual agents and international humanitarian organisations and the stories they are willing and/or able to take on board. The last line tells us that the jumble of such 'facts' and political conjecture combined to allow the global powers-that-be to consign the Sudanese question to the familiarly labelled dustbin of 'messy tribal conflict.' As I write, events in the Democratic Republic of Congo are hitting the international headlines. Once more, the global community confronts the literally life-and-death fallout from the fact that such complex political narratives refuse to adhere to the generic plotline and logic of black/white, good/evil, hero/villain, us/them. All roads, it seems, lead us back to Said.

'The Lure of the East' exhibition closed in August 2008. Revisiting the web-site the following month, I stumbled across a link advertising an online auction for a painting by Enzie Shahmiri, entitled 'Sudanese Girl.' Bidders were assured of the benevolent principles behind the sale, with all proceeds going to the United Nations to '[benefit] the people of Darfur.'[32] On her website, Shahmiri describes herself as a 'professional portrait artist and Orientalist painter.'[33] In conclusion, I re-view her 'Sudanese Girl' using the following excerpt:

> '[Achor Achor] finds something of interest and shows me a newsmagazine with a cover story about Sudan. A Darfurian woman, with cracked lips and yellow eyes, looks into the camera, at once despairing and defiant. Do you know what she wants, Julian? She is a woman who had a camera pushed into her face and she stared into the lens. I have no doubt that she wanted to tell her story, or some version of it. But now that it has been told, now that the countless murders and rapes have been documented, or extrapolated from those few reported, the world can wonder how to approach Sudan's violence against Darfur.'[34]

Whilst portraiture and photography are distinct mediums, a certain passivity is implied and employed by Shahmiri's painting and the iconic image of the Darfurian woman. Whether holding paint-brush or digital camera, it is arguable that the artist or photographer assumes control in both situations. As the loaded use of 'pushed' here suggests, a certain denial of agency and voice inevitably takes place.

As I have maintained throughout this chapter, debates about the politics and poetics of representation and reception are fundamental to *What is the What*. Whilst the novel is not primarily about Darfur, the focus of this passage seems indicative of the work as a whole. Reading *What is the What* in our current geo-political context, perhaps the most fundamental, trenchant questions it poses are, what stories are we willing to listen to, from who, how and where? Attempting to formulate answers is necessarily difficult. Yet, in the process of acknowledging and accepting this challenge, we undergo a transformative literary and critical thinking experience. The catalyst for producing *What is the What* was the desire to tell different stories about Sudan and its conflicts. In the midst of scholarly debates about literature, we can lose sight of the material conditions and political realities with which it engages. This salutary novel refocuses our attention on these subjects, rather than allowing us to divert our eyes. Rather than offering an escape-route from reality, such committed fiction can open a transformative window onto it.

Money generated from the sale of *What is the What* is currently being used to fund building projects in Deng's home village of Marial Bai. These include "a teacher-training college, a women's educational and vocational center and a public library."[35] From an individual book to a community library, *What is the What* offers a timely reminder of the power of literature, language and communication at both individual and collective levels. This recalls Aimé Césaire's omni-pertinent phrase: "exchange is oxygen."[36] It remains as applicable and essential to relationships between seemingly distinct times and spaces as it is to the enabling, productive, artistic partnership between Deng and Eggers. *What is the What* is a provocative work that seeks to enhance critical awareness by promoting humanistic exchange. As such, it stays true to the principles of Saidian thought:

> 'My idea ... is to use humanistic critique to open up the fields of struggle, to introduce a longer sequence of thought and analysis to replace the short bursts of polemical, thought-stopping fury that so imprison us in labels and antagonistic debate whose goal is a belligerent collective identity rather than understanding and intellectual exchange ... humanism is sustained by a sense of community with other interpreters and other societies and periods: strictly speaking ... there is no such thing as an isolated humanist.'[37]

President Obama has outlined a 'Yes, we can' vision for the United States and the world. If it is to prevail, perhaps we must all draw strength from the vital guidance offered by these lines.

References

Adams, Tim. 'A Lost Boy Who Found His Voice,' *The Observer*, 20.5.07

Césaire, Aimé (1972), *Discourse on Colonialism* [1955]. Trans. Joan Pinkham, New York: Monthly Review Press.

Eagleton, Terry (2005), *Holy Terror*, Oxford: Oxford University Press.

Eggers, Dave (2007), *What is the What: The Autobiography of Valentino Achak Deng* New York: Vintage Books.

Eggers, Dave (2000*)*, *A Heartbreaking Work of Staggering Genius*, New York: Simon and Schuster, 2000.

Gourevitch, Philip (2000), *We Wish to Inform You That Tomorrow We Will be Killed With Our Families: Stories from Rwanda*, London: Picador.

Huggan, Graham (2001), *The Postcolonial Exotic: Marketing the Margins* (London: Routledge.

Kakutani, Michiko. 'Lost Boy of Sudan Searching for a Land of Milk and Honey,' *The New York Times*, 7.11.06.

Kesey, Ken (1999), *One Flew Over the Cuckoo's Nest* [1962], New York: Penguin.

MacNeil, Kevin. 'A Boy's Own Story,' *The Sunday Herald*, 2.6.07

Peterson, Scott (2001), *Me Against My Brother: At War in Somalia, Sudan, and Rwanda*, London: Routledge.

Prose, Francine. 'The Lost Boy,' *New York Times Book Review*, 24.12.06.

Said, Edward W. (1994), *Culture and Imperialism*, London: Vintage.

Said, Edward W. (2003), *Orientalism* [1978], London, Penguin.

Spivak, Gayatri Chakravorty (1999), *A Critique of Postcolonial Reason: Toward a History of the Vanishing Present*, Cambridge, Mass: Harvard University Press.

Internet Sources

www.enzieshahmiri.com/artistbio

www.guardian.co.uk

www.portlandmercury.com

www.powells.com/biblio/1932416641

www.tate.org.uk/britain/exhibitions/britishorientalistpainting

www.valentinoachakdeng.org

www.world-market-portraits.blogspot.com/2008/04/fundraiser-looking-for-help

Notes

1. Terry Eagleton, *Holy Terror* (Oxford: Oxford University Press, 2005) p.85.
2. Dave Eggers, *What is the What: The Autobiography of Valentino Achak Deng* (New York: Vintage Books, 2007) p.142. All subsequent references to this edition.
3. In Philip Gourevitch, *We Wish to Inform You That Tomorrow We Will be Killed With Our Families: Stories from Rwanda* (London: Picador, 2000) p.238.
4. Edward W. Said, *Orientalism* [1978] (London, Penguin: 2003) p.xxvii.
5. See www.tate.org.uk/britain/exhibitions/britishorientalistpainting
6. Eggers, pp.525-526.
7. Dave Eggers, *A Heartbreaking Work of Staggering Genius* (New York: Simon and Schuster, 2000)
8. See www.portlandmercury.com/portland/Content?oid=78999&category=22148
9. See www.valentinoachakdeng.org
10. Graham Huggan, *The Postcolonial Exotic: Marketing the Margins* (Routledge, London: 2001) p.xiv.
11. Edward Said, *Culture and Imperialism* (Vintage, London: 1994) p.19.
12. Eggers, p.9.
13. Francine Prose, 'The Lost Boy,' *New York Times Book Review*, 24.12.06.
14. Michiko Kakutani maintains "the book is flawed by an odd decision on Mr. Eggers's part to fictionalize Mr. Deng's story." Interestingly, however, he goes on to concede, "it is a testament to the power of Mr. Deng's experiences and Mr. Eggers's ability to convey their essence in

visceral terms that we gradually forget these schematics of composition." 'Lost Boy of Sudan Searching for a Land of Milk and Honey,' *The New York Times*, 7.11.06.

15 Eggers, p.238.

16 See www.powells.com/biblio/1932416641

17 I write immediately after Barack Obama's announcement as the next President of the United States. A man of Kenyan descent, his acceptance speech seems peculiarly resonant in this context: "our stories are singular, but our destiny is shared." For the full transcript, see www.guardian.co.uk.

18 See Gayatri Chakravorty Spivak, *A Critique of Postcolonial Reason: Toward a History of the Vanishing Present* (Cambridge, Mass: Harvard University Press, 1999) pp.269-311.

19 Kevin MacNeil, 'A Boy's Own Story,' *The Sunday Herald*, 2.6.07

20 Tim Adams, 'A Lost Boy Who Found His Voice,' *The Observer*, 20.5.07

21 Eggers, p.xiv.

22 Eggers, p.xiv.

23 Eggers, pxv.

24 Eggers, p.xv.

25 Eggers, p.535.

26 Eggers, p.138.

27 Eggers, p.139.

28 Eggers, p.21.

29 See Scott Peterson's introduction to *Me Against My Brother: At War in Somalia, Sudan, and Rwanda* (London: Routledge, 2001) pp.xi-xxii.

30 Eggers, p.349.

31 Francine Prose has likened *What is the What* to *The Adventures of Huckleberry Finn*, calling the former "a picaresque novel of adolescence,' 'The Lost Boy,' New York Times Book Review, 24.12.06. An alternative, if equally provocative, American literary comparison might be Ken Kesey's *One Flew Over the Cuckoo's Nest* [1962] (New York: Penguin, 1999): "But it's the truth even if it didn't happen," p.7.

32 www.world-market-portraits.blogspot.com/2008/04/fundraiser-looking-for-help.html

33 www.blogger.com/profile/13959938138147453529 or www.enziesha hmiri.com/artistbio.htm

34 Eggers, pp.249-250.

35 Eggers, p.539.

36 Aimé Césaire, *Discourse on Colonialism* [1955]. Trans. Joan Pinkham (New York: Monthly Review Press, 1972) p.11.

37 Said, 2003 Preface to *Orientalism*, p.xvii.

Chapter 15

FICTIONAL WORKS OF AYI KWEI ARMAH AS A BASIS FOR DEMOCRACY AND RECONSTRUCTION IN WEST AFRICA

Anna Chitando

Introduction

African creative writers have been ignored in discourses on peace-building and development. African politicians, social scientists, technocrats and other experts have arrogated the responsibility to find solutions to the continent's manifold problems. Although some politicians in Zimbabwe have adopted the more politically correct term "challenges", Africa's problems remain urgent. These include gripping poverty, violence, HIV and AIDS, corruption and a host of other ills. The problems cut across the social, political, economic and spiritual domains. Africa's problems threaten the continent's celebration of independence.

By paying little or no attention to the contribution of creative writers, African politicians are missing the insights that this particular category of thinkers are making to the recreation of the continent. Of course, there have been instances when politicians have paid attention by harassing, imprisoning and even murdering African artists who have painted visions of a new Africa. Equally, other African intellectuals have charged that creative writers are "day dreamers" who envisage a "new heaven and a new earth" during our lifetime. They accuse them of indulging in hallucinations where they mystically see an egalitarian, peaceful society wherein every citizen enjoys life. That society is not possible in this life, critics charge.

This chapter utilises the case of the Ghanaian author, Ayi Kwei Armah, to highlight the contribution of creative writers to the imagination and pursuit of a new Africa. It is informed by Okot P'Bitek's (1986) argument that artists play an important role in African society. As Achebe (1988) maintained, it is the artist who can inform her or his society when its problems mounted and suggest possible solutions. Africa's spectacular failures in different areas are attributable to both internal and external factors. However, the failure of imagination emerges as the most prominent reason. If the continent would listen to its female and male artists, a better society would emerge.

Violence in the Postcolony: Armah's Diagnosis

The struggle for political independence in Africa had been described as a heroic struggle that prefigured the coming down of showers of blessings on the continent. African political leaders were presented as miracle workers who ushered in the dawn of a new era.

In Malawi, Dr Hastings Kamuzu Banda, was described as a highly intelligent and indispensable individual who availed limitless possibilities to his people. Religious symbols were used, deifying him in the process (Muyebe and Muyebe, 1999). In Zimbabwe, President Robert Mugabe has been described by some of his followers as "the son of God" or a black Moses who delivers the Holy Land to his people. In short, hopes have been high that the arrival of independence would transform the continent into paradise. But creative writers like Armah are not as optimistic.

Armah is a perceptive social commentator whose diagnosis of postcolonial Africa's problems is incisive. Born in 1939 in Ghana and educated at Achimota College, he proceeded to the United States where he studied sociology at Harvard. He taught African literature and creative writing at the College of National Education, Chang'ombe, Tanzania, from 1972 to 1976. He has also taught at the Universities of Massachusetts (1970) and Wisconsin (1979) in the United States. Armah has done scriptwriting, translating and editing. His artistic works include *The Beautyful Ones are Not Yet Born* (1968), *Fragments* (1969), *Why Are We So Blest?* (1972), *Two Thousand Seasons* (1973), *The Healers* (1979) and *Osiris Rising* (1995). Armah's stature as a leading African author has been confirmed by the number of books and journal articles that focus on his work.

Armah is an African intellectual with a keen sense of history. In his analysis of postcolonial Africa's situation, he draws attention to the plunder of the continent's resources by Europeans and Arabs. However, he does not fall into the trap of exonerating contemporary Africans and their leaders. He finds them culpable of intolerance, bad governance and lacking in imagination. The disillusioning realities of postcolonial politics and economics form the basis of Armah's work. The consumerism that characterises the continent's ruling elite frustrates Armah. It is this birth of a class of petty accumulators that he attacks. This comes out in his portrayal of the railway freight clerk in *The Beautiful Ones Are not Yet*

Born. Alongside other writers whose works appeared in the 1960s and 1970s, Armah envisages a revolution where new values are inculcated. In the words of one critic:

> In many of these novels, a preoccupation with political corruption and consumer capitalism is mediated through images of the consumption of food, eating, bodily decay and defecation (Innes, 1995: 1).

Armah's *The Beautyful Ones Are Not Yet Born* describes the violence that has gripped Ghanaian society after the attainment of independence. It is the same violence that Achebe explores in *A Man of the People* (1966), when political leaders engage in bloody games to gain political mileage. Often, images of naked physical violence are more effective in inducing a sense of shock. As a result, images of bodies floating in the river following the genocide in Rwanda, or amputated arms after the civil war in Sierra Leone, remain etched in one's consciousness. Global media networks are very good at using these powerful images to express the horror that is experienced in Africa. Armah's images are more subtle, but equally effective in highlighting the decadence that is found in postcolonial Africa.

In *The Beautyful Ones*, Armah is devastating in his exposition of psychological violence in independent Ghana. Unfulfilled hopes and aspirations have given rise to a society that is not at peace with itself. The socialist rhetoric does not reflect the reality on the ground. Freedom continues to be denied to citizens. The ruling elite remain suspicious of those who hold contrary views. Worse still, unbridled consumerism is their guiding ideology, despite their claims to follow socialist principles.

The main character, simply called 'the man,' representing the faceless masses, ponders whether this is the meaning of independence. He shares his pessimism with the Teacher. It is the Teacher who verbalises the author's frustration with the ruling elite:

> Life has not changed. Only some people have been growing, becoming different, that is all. After a youth spent fighting the white man, why should the president discover as he grows older that his real desire has been to be like the white governor himself, to live above all blackness in the big old slave castle (92).

Although Armah is frustrated with Nkrumah's corrupt and decaying regime, his insights are generally applicable to other African contexts. It is ironic that freedom fighters have practically become fighters against freedom (hence freedom fighters). In many instances, it has been a case of replacing white administrators with black faces. The violence against citizens, who are regarded as subjects (Mamdani, 1996), continues unabated. The same pieces of colonial legislation are used as instruments of surveillance. Is it not ironic that Mugabe, a convincing anti-colonial orator, used colonial legislation to demolish houses in urban areas in Zimbabwe during his "Operation Murambatsvina/Restore Order"? This underlines the contradictions and violence experienced in postcolonial Africa.

In Armah's narrative, the cycle of consumption, waste and disposal is indicative of the ruling elite's consumption patterns. The wastefulness of the ruling elite leads to violence at various levels. Ordinary citizens undergo profound soul-searching as their lived experiences do not reflect the hopes they had. A lingering question remains: "Is this what we fought for?" Some begin to long for the colonial period, asking, "When will independence be over so that we can begin to eat well again?" Such a society experiences untold psychological violence. Deflated aspirations and unmet expectations lead to suffering amongst the populace. Armah's work vividly describes such frustration.

For Armah, only a thorough "cleansing" and "rebirth" can give rise to a revitalised Africa. In *The Beautyful Ones*, Koomson's rescue by 'the man' is by way of a latrine hole and the back lanes and sewers leading to the sea and escape boat. Images of decay and excretion characterise the prevailing situation. Water, the universal symbol for rebirth, is used to represent the dawn of a new era. Violence, corruption and decay will be swept away when the second revolution gets underway. This revolution will rid society of its tensions and create a society based on mutual respect, gender equity and progress.

In his works, Armah is convinced that postcolonial Africa's problems are indelibly tied to the continent's refusal to define itself outside inherited Western values and systems. As long as Africans remain within the parameters set by the colonial mindset, there can be no progress or liberation. His political skepticism informs him that the contemporary African ruling elite is incapable of taking Africa where it rightly deserves to be. Furthermore, the Western education system continues to peddle untruths about the continent and its potential. History becomes fiction and fiction becomes history as Armah tries to awaken the continent. Ideologically, he positions himself firmly within the strand of Pan-Africanism.

Peace and development in Armah's works are the outcome of a continent coming to terms with its true self. Violence is not only the result of gunfire, machetes and other weapons of war. It is equally the result of restlessness within the body politic. It is the outworking of deferred dreams and unfulfilled promises.

Armah's characters show that psychological violence is as vicious as physical violence. The tragedy is that in postcolonial Africa both forms of violence are being experienced on a daily basis.

Armah's Vision: A Critical Analysis

Although creative writers have the license to dream and recreate society, such visions stand to be interrogated. Armah's quest for a new Africa that is rid of the impurities of Western consumerism and knowledge systems is quite appealing. His African consciousness that comes across in *Two Thousand Seasons* is quite acute.

However, Armah regresses into essentialism when he reconstructs Africa's story. As his compatriot, African philosopher Kwame Anthony Appiah (1992) argues, Africa is a multivalent concept. Armah operates with an essentialist reading of the continent. This can be seen in his proposal that Africans go back to "the way" or indigenous spirituality, while abandoning Christianity and Islam. He overlooks the fact that these religions have been embraced by millions of Africans who have, in turn, indigenised or Africanised them. It is no longer convincing to argue that African Christianity and African Islam are "foreign religions." They have become part of African identity.

The writer's preoccupation with the land of Africa has a strong ideological appeal. Land gives people a sense of belonging. However, some African politicians like Mugabe (2001), have used the land issue to evoke strong emotions while strengthening their grip on power. Furthermore, it might restrict Africans from settling in different other parts of the world. If people from other continents have decided to settle in Africa, why should the opportunity to settle elsewhere be denied to Africans? Armah's emphasis on a unique African identity might prevent his readers from appreciating that Africans share a lot in common with other races.

In his quest to create a new society, Armah's pessimism gets the better of him. One can accept that there are too many things that are wrong in Africa today. There are many leaders who continue to reflect a colonial mentality. There is massive corruption and rottenness on the continent.

However, this is not the complete story of Africa. There is also sweet smelling perfume on the continent. Despite massive problems, Africa is not a failed continent. Genuine peace obtains in many countries and happiness is carried in millions of hearts. Real progress has been attained in some African countries.

Armah's pessimism is needed to awaken the continent from a deep slumber. A new sense of optimism is needed to ensure that Africans work for peace and prosperity.

Conclusion

Armah is a visionary intellectual who refuses to celebrate independence uncritically. With other creative writers, he exposes the fault-lines and contradictions in African societies. Artists like Armah are urgently needed to sharpen conversations around violence, conflict and peace in Africa. Their dreams, visions and even hallucinations can fire the imagination. Their reconstructions, though based on fantasy, inform us that another world is possible. Contributors from other disciplines need to listen carefully to the vision enunciated by writers like Armah. Peace, perfect peace, becomes possible when individuals and communities dream. We become better when we cherish and interrogate such dreams.

References

Armah, Ayi Kwei (1968), *The Beautyful Ones Are Not Yet Born*. London: Heinemann.

___(1969), *Fragments*. London: Heinmann.

___(1972), *Why Are We So Blest?* New York: Doubleday.

___(1973), *Two Thousand Seasons*. Nairobi: East African Publishing House.

___(1978), *The Healers*. Nairobi: East African Publishing House.

___(1995), *Osiris Rising: A Novel of Africa Past, Present and Future*. Popenguine: Per Ankh.

Achebe, Chinua (1966), *A Man of the People*. Ibadan:Heinemann

___(1988), *Hopes and Impediments: Selected Essays*. London: Heinemann.

Appiah, Kwame A. (1992), *In My Father's House: Africa in the Philosophy of Culture*. New York: Oxford University Press.

Innes, C. Lynn (1995), "Conspicuous Consumption: Corruption and the Body Politic in the Writing of Ayi Kwei Armah and Ama Ata Aidoo," in Abdulrazak Gurnah (ed.), *Essays on African Writing*. Vol. 2. Contemporary Literature. 1-18. Oxford: Heinemann Educational Publishers

Mamdani, Mahmood (1996), *Citizen and Subject: Contemporary Africa and the Legacy of Late Colonialism*. Princeton: Princeton University Press.

Mugabe, Robert G. (2001), *Inside the Third Chimurenga: Our Land is Our Prosperity*. Harare: Department of Information and Publicity, Office of the President and Cabinet.

Muyebe, Stanslous and Alexander Muyebe (1999), *The Religious Factor within the Body of Political Symbolism in Malawi, 1964-1994*. Florida: Universal Publishers.

P'Bitek, Okot (1986), *Artist the Ruler: Essays on Art, Culture and Values*. Nairobi: Heinemann Kenya.

Chapter 16

ENGAGING THE DEAF THROUGH SONG AND POETRY: THE DILEMMA OF THE NIGERIAN ARTIST IN A SEASON OF POLITICAL ANOMIE

Hope Eghagha

How do we communicate bereavement of father and mother to a deaf and dumb prodigal son? How do we compel the leadership class, the current politicians to listen to the distilled wisdom of poetry and song? Shall we resort to exaggerations and caricatures to achieve our objectives?

For us and where we come from, deafness is a malady bad in itself. It can only be compounded by being in the leadership class. These are appropriated as metaphors for the state of politics in my birthplace.

'They will not listen', 'Do they read poetry? are apt summaries of the predicament of the writer. *'They'* represents the others, set apart by their access to political power and economic wealth. Fundamental contradictions are explained away in bland terms.

How does a writer become the announcer of death to the deaf political class? As the bereaved is culturally obliged to take note of the time and rites of passage of his parents, so too is the writer obliged to make this pronouncement to the government of the day. At what cost?

Why has the resonance of poetry and beauty escaped the eyes and minds of the current political office holders? How could they have forgotten history so soon? What other traditional methods may we adopt in a postcolonial world to draw attention to madness that governs the land?

The metaphor of the poet-writer communicating news of the death of the parents of the deaf to him as a vehicle for conveying the relationship between the political class and writers in Nigeria bears ambivalence which we ought to grapple with from the outset. We may pose this in the form of questions. What natural or unnatural occurrence inflicts an individual in the leadership class with the physiological burden of deafness? How does the victim cope with the existential challenges of the times? Why does a political system produce deaf men and women in the corridors of power? Why are Nigerian, indeed, African, politicians insensitive to the plight of the people they pretend to serve?

The headline of a Nigerian newspaper *This Day* of 23rd November 2006 quoted the Speaker of the House of Representatives (the lower arm of the legislature), Alhaji Aminu Masari, as saying:

"Nigerians need a listening President that would meet their needs and yearnings".

The general notion in the country currently is that Nigeria has a president who does not listen to the voice of reason. He carries on with the posture of a messiah, sent to save the country from the cesspit of corruption which the nation has found itself in. Perhaps this is typical of the average African leader, just as Ayi Kwei Armah points out in *The Beautyful Ones Are Not Yet Born* (1968: 86) when Manaan reflects on the Osagyefo thus:

I stood there staring like a believer at the man, and when he stopped

I was ashamed and looked around to see if anybody had been watching

me. They were all listening. The one up there was rather helpless-looking

with a slight, famished body. So from where had he got his strength that

enabled him to speak with such confidence to us, and we waiting patiently

for more to come? Here was something more potent than mere words. These

dipped inside the listener, making him go with the one he spoke.

……

Near the end he spoke about himself. If he could have remained that way!

But now he is up there, above the world, a saviour with his own worshippers,

Not a man with equals in life.

We refer to the arts generally as poetry and song, that aspect of aesthetics that thrill or reach the auditory sense of the human being. Poetry is profound, deep, meant for the soul of the reflective mind, the listening ear. It is meant for those who read the mind, whose vision reach beyond the mundane, the ordinary. The deaf refer to the human being who refuses or fails to appreciate the thematic concerns of the works of writers. Specifically, deafness is used metaphorically to depict the political class.

Engaging the political class through art, through poetry and song, is not a new experience in the Nigerian context. Wole Soyinka's *A Dance of the Forests*, *Kongi's Harvest*, Achebe's *A Man of the People* and *Anthills of the Savannah*, J.P. Clark's *Ozidi* and *Casualties*, Okigbo's *Labyrinth*, Osofisan's *Morountodun*, Iyayi's *Violence* and *Heroes*, Okey Ndibe's *Arrows of Rain*, are past attempts to hold a dialogue with leaders who do not read poetry or listen to songs of 'sorrow'.

It is perhaps foolhardy to attempt a conversation with a man who is predisposed to locked or sealed mental processes. The African proverb, 'a naked man who runs after a mad man for stealing his clothes will be taken for the mad man', may be apposite here. If we accept its import, it would be a signpost to inertia, to self-inflicted incapacitation.

The writer himself would become like his politician partner.

We recognise the capacity of the impaired person to get on in life, not weighed down by physical challenges. In other words, in literal terms, a deaf person is not necessarily a liability to society. Impaired persons who correctly identify the root of their problems are often able to rise above the strictures or impediments imposed by such a lack. There are available tools to aid the deaf perform his functions. These tools are available to physically-challenged persons who need them, are aware of their existence, and can afford them. The class of persons we have in mind here have the resources to buy the tools, know that they are available but simply reject the facilities.

In the adopted metaphor, the deaf are crippled by greed, lack of respect for the nuances of democracy, corruption, and avarice. They are the men and women in power.

The writer in Nigeria has certain social obligations thrust on him by reason of his position as a respectable and credible force in a society that is dominated by warped moral values. The African proverb, '*if you watch your neighbour eat cocoyam in the evening and you fail to warn him about the danger, you will be compelled to wake up in the night to treat him for stomach pain,*' captures the responsibility of the writer. As a member of the elite class he stands in a position to make comments on the state of affairs of things in the land. Osofisan (2001: 107-8) observes that 'it is the mouth of the artist that invariably leads him or her to a successful or tempestuous career, particularly in what has come to be known nowadays as 'the postcolonial state'.

Okigbo alludes to this in *'Hurrah for Thunder'* (67) when he says:

If I don't learn to shut my mouth I'll soon go to hell,

I, Okigbo, town-crier, together with my iron bell

He may not be wealthy, in fact, he is often not a man of wealth, but he has a moral stature in society which compels the government to listen to him. His 'big mouth' could also get him into trouble, a two-edged sword in the hands of the 'others', those outside the experience of deep poetic convictions.

Kofi Anyidoho (1997:5) dwells on this when he ruminates on the dilemma bird of Akan mythology. Santrofi, the bird:

> "is both a blessing and a curse...a blessing for the clarity of its vision and for the transforming beauty and power of its gift of song. But ...also a curse for its irritating and irrepressive urge to expose the unsavoury side of society".

The writer-activist is in greater danger in a postcolonial state. It is for this reason that Wole Soyinka went to jail in the late 1960s. Since then, the Nigerian state has passed through several military administrations and is now in the hands of a supposedly elected government.

The repetitive cycle of waste and wantonness in the African polity is captured by Ayi Kwei Armah in *The Beautyful Ones Are Not Yet Born* when he condemns the aftermath of the coup in the expression:'old music, new dance.'

In Achebe's *A Man of the People*, the economist who advises against printing more currency notes to meet expenditure is disgraced from government. His sound advice falls on deaf ears. In spite of the claims of the new, the vestiges of the old remain permanently glued to the contemporary, the present. It offers a picture of doom, this Sisyphean return to the mess of history, without the will to reverse the fortune of the people. It is not the insufficiency or unavailability of natural resources that causes it. It is the imposed will of inertia, a predisposition to neglect the fundamentals and chase the shadows of existence.

In the words of Toni Morrison, it *'is not a message to pass on'*. Yet it is the fact of contemporary history which we deal with in my place of birth.

The current reforms of the Nigerian government have not impacted on the region where I come from. The Niger Delta remains a tender spot in relations between the regions and the Federal Government. Polluted rivers, fragmented souls and a desperate polity all contribute to a feeling of despair. Poems and critical writing have failed to draw attention to the plight of the region. There is deafness everywhere, even among locally elected officials of state. These are accountable only to their masters in the federal capital, not to the people who elected them to office.

The current reign of violence is antithetical to peace and stability. But when the people have been pushed to the wall, they are capable of reacting in a manner that could disrupt the entire society. Their lives have been disrupted by many years of oil exploration anyway.

The 1999 Constitution of the Federal Republic of Nigeria guarantees freedom of expression to all. This fundamental requirement of the democratic culture also requires the state to provide security for the man who expresses his views even against the state. Sadly, we currently grapple with several cases of unresolved murders of people from the political class.

A serving Attorney-General, a chieftain of a political party, and two governorship candidates have been murdered in the last seven years. Two journalists were charged in court for sedition. The public outcry made the government soft-pedal.

Freedom of speech is a threat to the freedom of the politician to exploit the purse of state and live like a lord of the manor. Freedom of speech endangers the freedom of the political class to make vacuous promises and rig the next elections. Thus, the proclamation of democracy is not synonymous with the entrenchment of democracy.

Not so long ago, reading the political handwriting on the wall, Soyinka called on Nigerians to get ready for a return to the trenches. Nigerians had fought the last military regime of General Sani Abacha from the trenches; so, if the current political office holders were going to deny Nigerians the benefits of democracy, it was time to get ready to do battle.

The ears of the deaf can be opened; the tongue of the dumb can be set free. This is only possible, however, when the victim of deafness realises and agrees to confront the consequences of his deficiency. It may be cynical to observe that the men and women in power do not read poetry, nor do they have the time to listen to songs. Okigbo's warning in *Hurrah for Thunder* (1971:67)

> The smell of blood already floats in the lavender-mist of the afternoon
> The death sentence lies in ambush along the corridors of power;
> And a great fearful thing already tugs at the cables of the open air,
> A nebula immense and immeasurable, a night of deep waters –
> An iron dream unnamed and unprintable, a path of stone

did not prevent the outbreak of hostilities in Nigeria in 1967. Yet we know that their minions read on their behalf and told them what they do want to hear. The African proverb, *'If you want to abuse a big and powerful or a deaf man to whom you have no direct access, tell it to his son,'* may be applicable and relevant in this direction. Certainly, the then military president, General Yakubu Gowon, did not read Wole Soyinka's play, *The Man Died*, before the book was banned from the Nigerian geographical space in the 1970s.

Directly or indirectly, therefore, the works of writers catch the attention of the ruling elite. They may not change; they may not create a new world order, but the works, like the proverbial testament, will testify against the rulers.

References

Achebe, Chinua (1984), *The Trouble with Nigeria*, Oxford: Heinemann.

Anyidoho, Kofi (ed) (1997), *The World Behind the Bars and the Paradox of Exile*, Evanston Illinois: Northwestern University Press.

Armah, Ayi Kwei (1968), *The Beautyful Ones Are Not Yet Born*, Ibadan: Heinemann.

Eghagha, Hope (2002), *This Story Must Not be Told*, Lagos: African Cultural Institute

Okigbo, Christopher (1971), *Labyrinths*, Ibadan: Heinemann.

Osofisan, Femi (2001), *Insidious Treasons – Drama in a Postcolonial State*, Ibadan: Opon Ifa Publishers.

wa Thiong'o, Ngugi (1981), *Writers in Politics*, London: Heinemann.

Chapter 17

REFLECTIONS ON *INYENZI*

Andrew Brown and Karin Samuel in Conversation[1]

Inyenzi: A Story of Love and Genocide, is written by South African Andrew Brown and was first published by himself in 2000, but after the acclaim and success of his second novel *Coldsleep Lullaby*, it was republished by Zebra Press in 2007. The story takes place against the backdrop of the 1994 Rwandan genocide, and deals with love, loyalty and the horror of the genocide. In August 2008 I conducted an e-mail correspondence with Brown about his novel. The following conversation reflects my attempt to analyze Brown's novel, and to specifically explore with the author the vexed subject of genocide as it is represented in his book.

Karin Samuel: In April 1994, Rwanda became the site of what is now considered to be one of the most efficient and appalling cases of mass murder in modern history. The genocide, lasting 100 days, claimed the lives of approximately 800,000 Rwandans, the victims comprised of Tutsis and moderate Hutus. As genocide is a crime against all humanity, it is imperative that a collective narrative memory of the trauma is constructed, and literature plays an important part in this construction. Narratives not only legitimate trauma by recording it, but in the process of writing, writers are effectively "translating [the] tragic experience – [of] the 1994 genocide of the Tutsis – into lasting symbols and representations" ("Art section: Keeping memory alive in Rwanda" 151). It is these symbols and representations that provide some form of access into the experience of the genocide, and in this way aid in the construction of a collective narrative memory. What's involved is to facilitate some level of identification and empathy by writing the absent witness into the plot. The unique aspects of narrative literature are recognized by the *Journal of Genocide Research* as "integral parts of the quest to probe the world of genocide" (Huttenbach 9). The use of narrative aids in imagining "aspects of genocide that may not be so easily conveyed by the historical narrative, or even interviews with survivors and perpetrators" (Feinstein 33); fictional narratives can thus provide a form of insight into the genocide that other accounts cannot.

The incessant need to understand the causes, underpinnings and effects of genocide is reflected in the abundance of theoretical, psychological, sociological and political works on the topic. Although immensely useful, these academic studies often fail to access the emotional and physical trauma experienced by individuals, and in this aspect narrative art plays a fundamental role as it provides an understanding "in a way that the theoretical discussions of the same issues cannot achieve" and which is not "accessible by other means" (Gagiano qtd. in Bell 110). Fiction enables readers to vicariously experience the genocide through identification with individual characters. This empathetic quality of narrative provides a unique point of entry into the genocide and can open up avenues that may aid the reader's attempt to come to terms with the trauma of the genocide.

Fictional narratives also fulfill society's obligation "to assure memory of genocide that will speak to future generations" ("Art Section: Keeping memory alive in Rwanda" 149), as according to Simon Norfolk, "forgetting is the final instrument of genocide" (qtd. in Feinstein 32). The dedication to remembering and constructing a collective memory is illustrated in the 1998 project "Rwanda: Writing so as not to forget". Noke Jedanoon, a Chadian writer, asked various African writers to write about Rwanda so as to "use [their] art, to use literature to render what we would see, hear and understand of post-genocide Rwanda" (Tadjo online)[2]. One of the writers in the project, Véronique Tadjo from Côte d'Ivoire, stated that the motivation was that "we can't continue to write as if nothing had happened" (online), emphasising the significant impact that the genocide should have on future narratives emerging on and from Africa. Although Andrew Brown's *Inyenzi: A Story of Love and Genocide* was not a result of this project, it also speaks to the role of literature in bearing witness to the trauma.

As a South African, Brown inhabits the position of an outsider to Rwanda and this effectively shapes his narrative and point of view. I asked Brown what drew him to this story, as both a South African and as a member of the world community, and what influenced him to set the narrative during the time of genocide.

Andrew Brown: During the mid-1980s, when I was still a teenager, I was detained as an activist under the State of Emergency and held in solitary confinement at Pollsmoor Prison. When I was released, I left the country to travel around southern and central Africa, in a way to find my bearings in what was a complex country and continent. My travels took me through Burundi. While in Bujumbura, I was fascinated by the beauty of the country and its people, but also by the underlying tension I felt. I camped in the front garden of a French professor, and every morning I was woken up by the sound of tramping boots and militant war-chants. Groups of soldiers ran in formation through the streets of Bujumbura every morning. It was supposedly simply a daily training exercise, but the intention was clear. It was an intimidating show of power by the ruling party. And it was effective.

One day I was tramping in the searing heat, walking with my backpack down a road through the forested hills of Burundi. Despite the incredible heat, a thick cloud formed overhead and pelted me with hailstones the size of golf balls. They stung my skin and shattered on the road. And then, as quickly as it had come, the clouds disappeared and the ice melted away. For me, that memory captures the tensions and bizarre contrasts not only of Burundi, but of South Africa. It seemed clear that – even then – the tension was unbearable and that something would have to break.

Karin Samuel: Despite the presence of the 1949 Geneva Convention Against Genocide, which obliges the League of Nations (since renamed the United Nations) to act when presented with a recognised case of genocide, the world failed to 'recognise' what was happening in Rwanda as genocide and instead claimed only that 'acts of genocide' were occurring. This effectively absolved the world community from their obligation to intervene, and this (lack of) political response to the Rwandan genocide directly resulted in the continuation of the killings. Furthermore, Niranyan Karnik states that "Western media portrayed the Rwandan conflict as a product of tribal factions" (614) with news reports describing the killing as "tribal bloodletting that foreigners were powerless to prevent", implying that "the world had little choice but to stand aside and 'hope for the best'" (Melvern 231). Despite the fact that "there were no headlines about genocide", there were countless "graphic reports about corpses piling up on the streets and news stories about the scale of the killing, but there was little explanation in the commentary" (Melvern 231). This served to propagate the Western myth that these killings were merely the result of centuries of tribal conflict in atavistic Africa, thereby aiding in their refusal to accept responsibility to intervene on behalf of the Rwandans at risk. According to UN Lieutenant-General Roméo Dallaire, "the international community, through an inept UN mandate and what can only be described as indifference, self-interest and racism, aided and abetted these crimes against humanity" (5).

The silence or inability to speak genocide in both political discourse and in media representation therefore directly contributed to the perpetuation of the genocide in Rwanda. Consequently, there is a need to now uncover those silences and to fill them with speech. This need drives literary representations of the trauma by non-Rwandan writers, who are – at least in part – expressing in their narratives a sense of collective guilt, insisting that the world community, those absent during the genocide, should come to terms with their role in the genocide. Some of these writers thus evoke guilt in readers, making them aware of their absence during the genocide, and the effect that this absence had on the continuation of the genocide. In effect, these writers are not only writing the trauma of the genocide, but also the trauma of a world community that watches from the outside and that must now come to terms with not acting, with remaining silent, and with the impact that this failure may have on Rwandan lives and their own humanity.

These writers are also trying to make sense of the incomprehensible through narrating it; they are trying to facilitate some sort of engagement with the genocide in an attempt to intellectualise the horror. According to Mohamed Adhikari, "in the case of the Rwandan genocide one is faced not merely with the task of explaining how and why the genocide occurred but, crucially, also with accounting for large-scale popular participation in the killing" (282). Writing about the genocide can thus be a way for the author to try and make sense of what happened and attempt to account for the various unique aspects of this genocide, such as the aforementioned mass participation of individuals. According to Brown, this "selfish" motive informs and shapes his narrative.

Andrew Brown: When I started to write *Inyenzi* (in about 1999), I located the story in Burundi. But the more research I did, the more I realised that the real tragedy lay just across the border in Rwanda. That story – despite its enormity – was simply not told in our (or anyone else's) media. I was so shocked and horrified by what I read that I moved the story and located it in Rwanda. As a result the story changed from one of love during a time of strife, to "a story of love and genocide".

Rwanda (and Burundi, Sarajevo, Georgia and countless other places in the world) is an example for me of what human beings are capable of, given the right (or horribly wrong) mix of circumstances and pressures. The stories from the Rwandan genocide include the most confusing and tragic: school teachers and nurses turning into killers, and then returning to their caring jobs once the carnage was over, priests and nuns turning victims over to the *interhamwe*, family members destroying one another.

That was what I hoped to capture in the book. As with any writing, to some extent it was a selfish attempt to try and make sense of the incomprehensible for myself.

Karin Samuel: The writing process itself then becomes a way to try and make sense of the incomprehensibility of the genocide. Part of this process involves the expression of the pain and trauma of the genocide. The difficulty of expressing pain and of translating trauma into language is explored by Elaine Scarry in *The Body in Pain: The Making and Unmaking of the World*. According to Scarry "physical pain has no voice" (3) as it "does not simply resist language but actively destroys it" (4). This is achieved through the recognition that physical pain "unlike any other state of consciousness – has no referential content" (5). Yet in order to represent trauma, it is vital to attempt to translate that pain into language so that it can be communicated to others and in this way enable the reader to bear witness to suffering. This is achieved partly through the use of symbols, metaphors and imagery; the efficacy and importance of figurative poetics lies in its ability to allow for subjective confrontation with the trauma, as readers become co-producers and decoders of the images.

The trauma of genocide is not only limited to physical pain, but also includes psychological suffering and emotional distress. These non-physical forms of pain also elude linguistic translation, and thus the question of how to write or represent suffering becomes a pressing concern to writers such as Brown, who are concerned to avoid a voyeuristic presentation of the pain of the other.

Andrew Brown: I am a person who shies away from depictions of suffering. I refuse to watch holocaust films. I watched *Hotel Rwanda* (and hated every minute of it), but refused to see any of the other films on the genocide. I cannot abide war movies. I cannot read books which detail the suffering of children; I will not read books (fact or fiction) which deal with rape, molestation or any other form of sexual abuse.

And yet *Inyenzi* focuses on a genocide that included the murder and mutilation (as a matter of course) of women and children. If *Inyenzi* had been written by someone else, there is no chance whatsoever that I would read it. And yet, having written it, the book remains far closer to my heart than anything else I have written subsequently – and not just because it was my first book to be published.

Karin Samuel: *Inyenzi* is the fictional story of Melchior, a Hutu priest, who is sent to work at a church in rural Bukumara after finishing his studies in Butare. It is whilst he is there that Tutsis, who are fleeing the deadly *interahamwe*[3], seek refuge in his church compound. One of these Tutsis is Selena, the woman Melchior fell in love with when he was studying, yet their love is forbidden not only by the church, but also by her position as a Tutsi, an *inyenzi*[4]. Melchior's presence at the compound, and the fact that the head of the communal police is his childhood friend, Victor Muyigenzi, grants those under his care a certain level of protection. But when Melchior is forced to leave the compound, in order to seek assurance from Colonel Batho (one of the more prominent *genocidaires* in the text) that those in his compound will be spared, the *interahamwe* proceed to slaughter them mercilessly in his absence.

It is through the characters that the reader is able to engage in a type of participatory understanding of the genocide. The two main characters of the novel, Melchior and Selena, draw the reader into the narrative on a most personal level and are, most notably, not immediately marked ethnically as Hutu and Tutsi. This approach restores the humanity of the victims as it humanises those that have been de-humanised in the genocide and who are now reduced to mere statistics and ethnic markers. The ability to gain access to the genocide through the point of view of individual characters is facilitated through the use of focalisation: a narrative technique that makes the reader privy to what is thought, felt and experienced by the character. As a result, the reader can reach some level of identification with the character/s and "through such identification, it is said, people transcend their limited personal experience" (Goldstein 189). This therefore engages the reader empathetically with both the characters and their situation, and ultimately with their suffering as well. Mohamed Adhikari advocates this stance when he states that "individual experiences can indeed be a most effective vehicle for illuminating broader social, even global, experiences and truths" (281). Characterization thus plays a fundamental role in the imaginative reconstruction of genocide.

Andrew Brown: The reason that *Inyenzi* is so important to me, and will always remain so, I suppose lies in its characters. The book was written almost entirely from a characterisation perspective. The characters could have been in Sarajevo, or Burundi, or South Africa. I chose Rwanda because it felt like the untold story: but the characters were paramount for me. It may seem glib to say that the characters wrote the story – but to some extent it is true. Unlike *Coldsleep Lullaby*[5], where the plot was worked out first and then the characters chosen to 'color in' between the lines, *Inyenzi* was all about characters. So much so (I reluctantly confess) that at times I thought I saw Melchior walking past me in the street.

The three central characters, Melchior, Selena and Victor, plus the additional characters of Gratian and Michel, were absolutely the centre of the book for me. I had these characters in my mind from the beginning, while the plot was far less certain. It was the love affair between Melchior and Selena that really drove the writing forward and determined how events unfolded.

However, being so character-centered made the writing of traumatic incidents far harder. The death of Michel was a horrible necessity – I needed to bring home the reality of the genocide and I knew (from the moment I created him) that it was inevitable that the likeable Michel would become a victim. But even as I created his death, I felt so terribly for him. The horror of what I was retelling in *Inyenzi* is what drove me to use this structure of the book…

Karin Samuel: Parallel to the narrative of Melchior, is the documentation on and legal proceedings of the International Criminal Tribunal for Rwanda, where Victor Muyigenzi is being tried for crimes against humanity for his involvement in the genocide, specifically the massacre at the church compound. Various documents – such as court transcripts, newspaper reports, press releases and witness statements – outlining his trial are alternated and interweaved with the story of Melchior. The novel thus unfolds in two separate, yet inextricably intertwined, semantic modes: the narrative space of the genocide in Rwanda in 1994 and the legal space of the judicial enquiry in Arusha, Tanzania in 1997.

The constant shift between these two spaces, between these different orders of representation, creates a third, unstable state from which new idioms might emerge. Francois Lyotard, the French philosopher and literary theorist, defines this third space as the 'differend': the "unstable state and instant of language wherein something which must be able to be put into phrases cannot yet be" (13). In the case of genocide, the trauma and pain of the atrocity becomes this 'differend' – that which cannot yet be put into language. In order to aid in constructing a collective narrative memory of the genocide, the trauma of the genocide must be translated in a way that makes it shareable, or at least partly so. Lyotard states that "This is when the human beings who thought they could use language as an instrument of communication learn through the feeling of pain which accompanies silences…, that they are summoned by language…to recognize that what remains to be phrased exceeds what they can presently phrase, and that they must be allowed to institute idioms which do not yet exist" (13). Lyotard thus suggests that ordinary language is inadequate for the expression of the differend, and that new idioms that do not yet exist need to be instituted in an attempt at expression. In *Inyenzi*, the third space that is created in the interplay between textual representation and the reader's imagination through the shift between discourses becomes the space where a new idiom can emerge that attempts to express the inexpressible: the horror of the Rwandan genocide.

Andrew Brown: The structure of the book is driven by the horror (for me as author) of its telling. The most acute example is the murder of Melchior, which was an unbearable scene to depict. I had invested so much of myself in him, I shared so much of him as a character and experienced his love of Selena so acutely, that his murder was simply not a scene that [I] could write in normal prose. To cope with this, I did two things. First, I removed myself from the scene so that I did not have to witness it myself: I made Selena the witness, and then protected her (and me) further by taking her away from the scene and having her hear the shot from across the valley, rather than actually see the killing taking place. And secondly, I placed the conclusion – the fact of his murder by Victor – in the formality of a Court document. That way, I spared myself the trauma of having to describe the scene. At the same time, it felt as if I managed to preserve the dignity of Melchior as a character: the record by the Court of his death lends a gravitas that I feel might be diminished if I were to describe his last moments. Death at the hands of another cannot realistically be described in a manner that affords dignity or strength to the victim. For that reason, Selena does not see it, Victor does not confess to its details and the Court is unable to describe it.

The murder of Melchior is the most extreme example, but the book uses this escape on a number of occasions. The death of Michel, the murder of Joseph, the carnage at the church, are all described through the medium of more removed documents and accounts.

My hope is that, in seeking to spare myself, I will also be sparing the reader. I do not think (or at least, I hope) that it makes the tragedy less powerful – if anything, relying on one's imagination may increase the power of the story told.

Karin Samuel: The legal documents that are used in the novel create distance between the reader and the trauma, through the use of detached, crisp, cold and unambiguous language. This is contrasted with the shift to narrative prose that, replete with figurative language, characterisation and focalisation, draw the reader in to a position of empathetic and participatory identification with the characters on an individual level. The nature of the prose, be it either legal or narrative prose, therefore determines whether the reader is detached from or drawn into the story. The mode of representation and the language used in that discourse consequently plays an important role in the reader's engagement with the novel.

While promising to bridge the gap between the reader and the genocide, language itself can also be a means of distancing, as experienced in the legal space created within the novel. At the same time, this distancing legalistic prose reflects to some extent the ways in which language was used by the perpetrators themselves in the genocide. The perpetrators made use of figurative language in order to distance themselves from their victims. The title of the novel, *Inyenzi*, is a Kinyarwandan term that literally means cockroach. The use of this term is significant not only in that it is Kinyarwandan (as opposed to English, in which the novel is written), but that it has specific interpretations and appropriations during and after the genocide. The perpetrators of the genocide used this term to refer to the Tutsis in order to de-humanise them and mark them as subjects deserving of death. It is a method of dehumanisation and humiliation that is not limited to the Rwandan genocide, but was present in the Holocaust as well where the victims were referred to as pigs. Labelling the victims as such effectively separates the self from the other, and "once the 'other' is sufficiently stigmatized and dehumanised, it becomes easy and even necessary for 'us' to massacre 'them' without any sense of guilt or remorse" (Odora 4-5). Reducing their victims to animals and pests, to beings that do not feel, think or act like 'we' do, perpetrators not only justified their behavior, but also satisfied their conscience. The reference to Tutsis as *inyenzi* not only marks them as vermin, pests and invaders to be systematically killed, but even identifies them as symptoms of an unhygienic disorder; their killing is thus naturalised as an act of cleaning out the (national) house. In labeling the Tutsis as cockroaches, the perpetrators are thus going further than merely distancing themselves from their victims: they are naturalising their own murderous behaviour as well.

Within the novel, the different levels or stages of dehumanising undergone by the victims is outlined by Melchior after he comes upon the mangled body of Joseph Gatagero, a suspected member of the Rwandan Patriotic Front (RPF). In his attempt to understand "the apparent ease with which a young man had been reduced to a crushed outline of thickened blood and flesh" (97), he comments on the process of dehumanisation that could lead to such behavior. He states that "No doubt it had made it easier, in principle, first to label their victim *icyitso* – an RPF supporter – not to call out his name, but to call him an *Inkotanyi* soldier, to accuse him of being a hater of Rwanda, part of the *inyangarwhanda*, and to denigrate him until he was no longer a person worthy of life but merely a nuisance, a parasite, *inyenzi*. Once he had been stripped of his human form, then perhaps the act became possible" (98-99).

Similarly, the use of the word "work" gains double meaning within the context of the genocide: besides the traditional denotation of harvesting or working in the fields, it was used as a metaphor for killing Tutsis. A machete that is used to harvest is a tool, but when used to kill a person it becomes a weapon. So it is the surface that the machete is used on that determines the function of the instrument. But in the case of the genocide, the perpetrators used machetes to kill people, using them as weapons, but claimed that they were 'working', thus "translating" the murderous machete back into a tool. This act of translation that takes place through figurative language changes how they view the surface that they are penetrating: instead of seeing their victims as human and their actions as killing, they are reducing them to objects and making their actions morally acceptable. Appropriating the word "work", the perpetrators distance themselves from the killing by associating their use of the machete with harvesting. According to Scarry, the use of the word "work" indicates the moral and mental distance that the perpetrators feel towards their victim, as they view the surface that is being penetrated as non-sentient (173), and therefore not human. This duplicity in the language is commented on by the character of Michel, a friend of Melchior's, when he says that "they [the perpetrators] use words differently…they talk about 'work', but they mean something else" (101).

Andrew Brown: You refer in your summary – with insight – to the issue of detachment and draw some parallels between the use of language in the book and the use of language in the perpetration of the genocide itself.

In the book, the description of the murder of Melchior in legalistic language makes the incident seem almost morally acceptable. Melchior becomes the subject of a legal inquiry and his death becomes one fact within that inquiry. It is a fact that bears equal importance with other facts: in truth, the most important fact becomes the guilt of the accused, not the death of the victim, which becomes a given. Language and register can quickly take the sting out of the reality of the meaning. Similarly, the book concentrates on the use of language during the genocide: the use of the word "inyenzi", phrases like "cutting the brush" and "coming out to work", these all diminish the reality of meaning. It amazed me that people who are prepared to wield machetes and kill others so brutally, still bother to couch their language in euphemism and code. But it allows them to detach from the reality of their victims as human: their conduct becomes 'work', the removal of 'vermin', a necessary evil. It is partly this detachment (but only partly, I think) that allows ordinary people to perpetrate the extraordinary acts of cruelty that have taken place in Rwanda and elsewhere around the globe.

Karin Samuel: *Inyenzi* provides the reader with a glimpse into the genocide and how the perpetrators used language to legitimise their behavior and dehumanise their victims. The distance created between victim and perpetrator through this appropriation of language is seemingly mirrored in the distance formed between reader and text through the detached tone of the legal discourse. In the narrative prose, however, the reader is drawn into the story through the characters and an empathetic response is elicited through identification with those characters. This restores the humanity of the victims and allows the reader to view the victims not as statistics, but as individuals. The attempt to represent suffering thus serves to highlight the trauma and horror of the genocide on an individual level and possibly aids in trying to avert such extreme acts of cruelty in the future by appealing to our inherent and common humanity.

References

Adhikari, Mohamed (2006), "*Hotel Rwanda*: too much heroism, too little history – or horror?" *Black and White in Colour: African History on Screen*. Eds. Vivian Bickford-Smith & Richard Mendelsohn. South Africa: Double Storey Books. 279-299.

Art Section, 2003, "Keeping Memory Alive in Rwanda". *Journal of Genocide Research* 5.1: 149-151.

Bell, Richard, H. (2002), *Understanding African Philosophy: A Cross-Cultural Approach to Classical and Contemporary Issues*. New York and London: Routledge.

Brown, Andrew (2005), *Coldsleep Lullaby*. Cape Town: Zebra Press.

Brown, Andrew (2007), *Inyenzi: A Story of Love and Genocide*. 2000. Cape Town: Zebra Press.

Dallaire, Romeo (2004), *Shake Hands with the Devil: The Failure of Humanity in Rwanda*. London: Arrow.

Diop, Boubacar Boras (2006), *Murambi, Book of Bones*. (Transl.), Fiona McLaughlin. Bloomington: Indiana University Press.

Feinstein, Stephen C. (2005), "Destruction has no covering: Artists and the Rwandan Genocide". *Journal of Genocide Research* 7.1: 31-46.

Goldstein, Jeffrey (1998), "Why we watch". *Why We Watch: The Attractions of Violent Entertainment*. Ed. Jeffrey Goldstein. New York & Oxford: Oxford University Press. 212-226.

Huttenbach, Henry R. (1999), "From the Editor: *Apologia Rationalis*". *Journal of Genocide Research* 1.1: 7-10.

Lyotard, Francois (1988), *The Different: Phrases in Dispute*. Minneapolis: University of Minnesota Press.

Makino, Uwe (2001), "Final solutions, crimes against mankind: on the genesis and criticism of the concept of genocide". *Journal of Genocide Research* 3.1: 49-73.

Melvern, Linda (2004), *Conspiracy to Murder: The Rwandan Genocide*. London & New York: Verso.

Scarry, Elaine (1985), *The Body in Pain: The Making and Unmaking of the World*. New York and Oxford: Oxford University Press, 1985.

Tadjo, Véronique (2004), *The Rwanda Forum*. 27 March. Website last accessed: 10 November 2007. Web site address: <http://london.iwm.org.uk/upload/package/33/rwanda/pdf/Veronique_Tadjo.pdf>

Tadjo, Véronique (2005), *The Shadow of Imana: Travels in the Heart of Rwanda*.

Trans. Véronique Wakerley. Cambridge: ProQuest Information and Learning Company.

Notes

[1] This conversation took place in the form of informal questions and answers via e-mail between Andrew Brown and Karin Samuel from 19 to 27 August 2008.

2   Véronique Tadjo's *The Shadow of Imana* and Boubacar Boris Diop's *Murambi, Book of Bones* are two novels that form part of this project.
3   Literally meaning "those who work together" or "those who fight together", the *interahamwe* were Hutu militia that was responsible for most of the killing during the 1994 genocide.
4   Literally means "cockroach".
5   *Coldsleep Lullaby* is Andrew Brown's second novel, published in 2006 by Zebra Press, and it was awarded the *Sunday Times* Fiction Prize in 2006.

NOTES ON CONTRIBUTORS

Lauryn Arnott was born in Zambia and educated in Zimbabwe and South Africa. While an art student in South Africa, she removed her drawing from the 1981 Republic Festival Exhibition in protest against Apartheid. In 1989, during another state of emergency in South Africa, she moved to independent Zimbabwe, married and had children. In 1994 President Robert Mugabe awarded her a prize for her picture called 'May Peace Prevail' – a memorial litho print about the Gukurahundi massacres. In 2003 she left Zimbabwe for Australia. In Adelaide, Arnott won the 2006 Association of Commonwealth Universities Prize in an exhibition entitled 'A Place in the World'.

David Bell is an independent scholar and authorised translator. He has been a Senior Lecturer in English Literature at Mid-Sweden University College and Head Department, and a Visiting Lecturer in English Literature at Lund University. Bell has also been a visiting Nordic Research Scholar at the NAI. Though now officially retired, he is into full time research and writing. He has published on British working-class fiction of the 1930s (*Ardent Propaganda*) and on contemporary South African fiction in English, mostly Zakes Mda. Apart from writing, he has organised and co-organised two conferences in Stersund (on Nation and Region and on Conrad) and published their proceedings and have co-convened a seminar (Riots in Literature) at the ESSE Conference in London, and contributed to ALA and EACLAS conferences. David Bell is currently co-editing a selection of essays on the works of Zakes Mda

Juliane Okot Bitek is the daughter of a poet father and a storyteller mother. She was born to exiled parents in Kenya, came of age in Uganda and now lives in Canada. Juliane is an award winning fiction writer, essayist and poet. She has a Bachelor's Degree in Fine Art (1995) from the University of British Columbia, Canada and is currently working on a memoir as she completes her graduate studies. *Words In Black Cinnamon: A Collection of Poetry* (Delina Press, Vancouver), was published in 1998. She is grateful to live with her husband and children in Vancouver.

Anna Chitando writes in the area of Gender Studies and Children literature. She is presently with the Zimbabwe Open University. Together with Ezra Chitando, she has written on: "Weaving Sisterhood: Women

African Theologians and Creative Writers", in *Exchange*, Volume 34, No.1, 2005. Her most recent publication is on: Imagining a Peaceful Society: A Vision of Children's Literature in a Post-Conflict Zimbabwe, *Nordic Africa Institute Discussion Paper*, 40, 2008.

Hope Eghagha is a poet, dramatist, and newspaper columnist. He is an Associate Professor and teaches Drama and Poetry at the Department of English, University of Lagos, Akoka Lagos, Nigeria. He has to his credit four poetry collections – *Rhythms of the Last Testament, This Story Must Not Be Told, The Governor's Lodge*, and *Premonitions*. He also has two plays, *Death, Not a Redeemer* and *Onowawi Shall Rise Again* and a novel, *Emperors of Salvation* that was published by Malthouse in 2003.

Kevin Eze was born in Nigeria in 1975. He grew up in Onitsha, Eastern Nigeria's largest commercial city, and began learning classical piano at the age of seven. He studied Philosophy and French at the Jesuit College in Kinshasa, Democratic Republic of Congo. He holds a Masters degree in Sociology from the University of Paris and currently lectures in the French curriculum of the National School of Arts of Dakar. He brings exhaustive research and penetrating insight to his upcoming book *Nigeria After 50*, to be published in 2009 by Raider Books, New York, USA.

Chenjerai Hove is a Zimbabwean, born near the mining town of Zvishavane, poet, novelist and essayist, he now lives in exile in Norway. He has published extensively during the past 25 years. Widely translated into many languages. Chenjerai has won several national and international literary awards, including the Zimbabwe Literary Award (1988) and the Noma Award for publishing in Africa (1989) for his novel, *Bones*. His other works include *Shadows*, a novel(1991), *Ancestors*, a novel (1997), Poetry anthologies, *Up in Arms* (1982), *Swimming in Floods of Tears* (1983), *Red Hills of Home* (1985), *Rainbows in the Dust* (1997), *Blind Moon* (2003), and journalistic\cultural essays *Shebeen Tales* (1989) *and Plaver Finish*(2002). In 2001, Chenjerai was awarded the German-Africa Prize for his contribution towards social justice and freedom of expression by the German-Africa Foundation, together with the German parliament.

Ogaga Ifowodo is a lawyer, and holds an MFA from Cornell University, New York, USA. He has published *Homeland & Other Poems*, which won the 1993 Association of Nigerian Authors (ANA) poetry prize; *Madiba*, winner of the 2003 ANA/Cadbury poetry prize; *The Oil Lamp*, winner of the 2003 ANA/NDDC Gabriel Okara poetry prize, and *Homeland*, a German-

English selection of his poems. He worked for eight years with the Civil Liberties Organisation (CLO), Nigeria's premier human rights group, and between 1997 and 1998 was held under preventive detention by the then military regime of Nigeria. A memoir of his prison experience, excerpts from which have been featured in *Gathering Seaweed: African Prison Writing* (ed. Jack Mapanje), the British Council and Granta's *New Writing 14*, and in Nigeria's *Vanguard* newspaper, is in progress. His poems have been widely published in anthologies and magazines, including: *Step Into a World: A Global Anthology of the New Black Literature, The Times Literary Supplement, The Massachusetts Review, The Dalhousie Review, Atlanta Review, Poetry International, Mantis, Drumvoices Revue*, among others. In 1998, he was named recipient of the PEN USA Barbara Goldsmith Freedom-to-Write Award and of the Poets of All Nations (Netherlands) "Free Word" Award. He is an honorary member of the PEN centres of the USA, Canada and Germany and a fellow of the Iowa Writing Program. He is currently concluding a doctorate in English at Cornell.

John Masterson teaches postcolonial studies, European literature and critical theory in the Department of Literature, Film, and Theatre Studies at the University of Essex, U.K. He has published chapters on the work of Nuruddin Farah and Chimamanda Adichie and is currently preparing a monograph entitled *The Disorder of Things: A Foucauldian Approach to the Work of Nuruddin Farah* for publication. His profile of the author will appear in *The Literary Encyclopedia* in 2009. His research interests include representations of African civil conflicts (particularly in relation to Somalia, Rwanda and Sudan), the work of J.M. Coetzee, and discourses surrounding the 'War on Terror.'

Munyaradzi Makoni is a freelance writer. His career spans 10 years. He has worked as a journalist in Zimbabwe as well as stringing for various international publications. He has previously worked as assistant editor for Moto Magazine. Denied by survival circumstances and armed with the priceless passion to write, he relocated to Cape Town in 2007. His articles in South Africa have appeared in *The Big Issue, The Southern Cross, The People's Post, Scientific Development Network* and *West Cape News*. In July 2008, he became a writer for Learning Cape, promoting lifelong learning. He is married with two children.

Okey Ndibe currently teaches fiction and African literature at Trinity College in Hartford, Connecticut in the United States of America (USA). He was a professor of English at Simon's Rock College in Great

Barrington, MA, USA. In 2002, he won the college's New Faculty Teaching Award. During the 2001-2002 year, Okey was a Fulbright Lecturing/Research Scholar at the University of Lagos, Nigeria. His novel, *Arrows of Rain,* has been praised by critics and authors, including the Nigerian-born 1986 Nobel laureate Wole Soyinka. The novel has been described by the Oxford, U.K-based *New Internationalist* magazine as "a powerful and gritty debut." The magazine also chose *Arrows of Rain* as one of the most remarkable new novels in its special October 2001 edition on "New Fiction from the South." Ndibe was the founding editor of *African Commentary,* a magazine published in the U.S. by novelist Chinua Achebe, author of the classic novel, *Things Fall Apart. African Commentary* was named by *Library Journal* as one of the 16 best new publications to come out in the U.S. in 1989. *USA Today, The Detroit Free Press, Utne Reader and Hampshire Gazette* (among others) also honoured the magazine as outstanding. He also served as a member of the editorial board of *Hartford Courant.* A piece he wrote in the Courant titled "Eyes to the Ground: The Perils of the Black Student," was chosen by the Association of Opinion Page Editors in 2001 as the best opinion piece published in any American newspaper. Another piece by him titled "Unwarranted Graphic Authentication," was named best opinion piece by the Society of Professional Journalists, Connecticut Chapter, for 2001. From 1997 to 2000, Okey was also a visiting professor of English and Creative Writing at Connecticut College in New London, Connecticut. He was named by the *College Voice,* the college's student newspaper, as one of the college's "Five Outstanding Professors." Okey writes for several publications in the U.S. and England, including *Hartford Courant, Transatlantimes Times, The Fabian Society Journal, Black Issues Book Review, BBC Online,* and Emerge. Since 1999, he has written a weekly column for The Guardian, widely regarded as Nigeria's stellar daily newspaper. He has just finished work on a novel titled, "foreign gods, inc." An excerpt from the novel is published online: www.guernicamag.com.

Thabisani Ndlovu was born in Lupane, Zimbabwe, on 22 December 1971. He holds a Masters Degree in English from the University of Zimbabwe, and is currently reading for a PhD on Zimbabwean writer Charles Mungoshi at The University of the Witwatersrand, South Africa. He has taught at school and lectured at University level, published short stories in various compilations and newspapers in Zimbabwe. He has also won several writing contests in Zimbabwe, the latest being first prize in the Intwasa ko Bulawayo Short Story Competition in 2005.

Yvonne Adhiambo Owuor has worked for three years as the Executive Director of the multi-arts Zanzibar International Film Festival. She is a published writer of fiction and non-fiction and recipient of the 2003 Caine Prize for African writing for Weight of Whispers (Kwani, 2003, Chimurenga 2003 and in 'A' is for Ancestors, 2004). She also received the 2004 Eve Woman of the year Award (Arts and culture Category). She has published several short stories, two of which have been optioned by film producers. She sits on different boards connected with conservation, culture, arts and skills exchange. Yvonne is also a UNESCO consultant involved with a film oriented ICT for Indigenous Peoples project in Laikipia, Kenya.

Karin Samuel is an alumnus of Stellenbosch University where she currently holds an Honours (Cum Laude) in English, and a teaching diploma in English Studies and Music. She is completing her Masters in English Literature with a thesis on texts concerning the Rwandan Genocide. Her Masters thesis is tentatively titled Rwanda and the Artist: Representations of Trauma in Narrative and the Construction of a Collective Narrative Memory. Her fields of academic interest include representations of violence and trauma, African literature, narrative memory and narrative theory, amongst others. She has been teaching first year students at the University for three years, and in 2009 will be the Assistant Course and Resource Coordinator for the first year English Course.

Skye Wheeler was born in Nairobi, Kenya and has spent most of her life in the region. She works as a freelance journalist in Juba, South Sudan.

Michael Woodman was raised and educated in Zimbabwe and undertook medical training at the University of Cape Town, South Africa, and further studies in Australia and the United Kingdom. He returned to Zimbabwe to work at a government hospital before embarking on a career in humanitarian medicine serving in conflicts or disasters ranging from Afghanistan, Sri Lanka, Indonesia, Democratic Republic of Congo, Sudan, and finally back to Zimbabwe. His passion is to provide good quality medical care for the most needy in a world of ever increasing inequalities. He lives in Harare with his partner Tanya.

INDEX

A

Abacha, Gen Sani, 50, 169
Abu Ghraib, 19
Achebe, Chinua, 27, 157, 159, 162, 167, 168, 170, 187
Acholi, 44, 46
Afrikaans English, 106
Afro-Scandinavian Writers' Conference, 49
AIDS, 43, 46, 65, 104, 157
Anglo-Saxon Protestant, 18
Apartheid South Africa, 19
Arnott, Lauryn, 107, 184
Association of Commonwealth Universities, 111, 184

B

Banda, Kamuzu, 158
Bell, David, 123, 131, 133, 172, 181, 184
Berger, John, 107
Biafra, 29, 30
Biko, Steve, 104
Bitek, Juliane Okot Bitek, 27, 43, 47, 157, 163, 184
Boro, Adaka, 50, 51
Brazzaville, 84
Brown, Andrew, 171, 172, 174, 175, 176, 178, 180, 181, 182, 183
Bulawayo, 58, 68, 126, 128, 187
Burundi, 172, 173, 174, 176

C

Cape Town, 101, 105, 124, 129, 132, 133, 181, 182, 186, 188
Chechnya, 19

Chidoro, Shelton, 39
China, 45
Chitando, Anna, 157, 184
Church-goers, 148
Civil Society, vii
Coetzee, J.M., 111, 186
Congo River, 81
Conrad, Joseph, 17, 20, 184
consumerism, 158, 159, 161
Côte d'Ivoire, 172

D

Dag Hammarskjöld Foundation, vii
Darfur, 9, 19, 31, 50, 69, 78, 142, 143, 151, 152
Democratic Republic of Congo, 10, 151, 185, 188
Diaspora, 43, 109, 111, 148

G

Gatagero, Joseph, 179
Ghana, 158, 159
Gowon, Yakubu, 52, 170
Guantanamo Bay, 19
Gukurahundi, 57, 58, 59, 63, 184

H

Hove, Chenjerai, vii, 11, 41

I

Ifowodo, Ogaga, 49, 185

J

Janjaweed, 69, 74

Index

K

Kampala Road, 44
Kasavuvu, 82, 83, 84, 86, 87, 88
Khartoum, 92, 94, 95, 96, 98, 99, 150
Kigali, 84
Kuac Ayok, 94

M

Masterson, John, 137, 186
Matabeleland, 57, 126, 127, 132, 133, 134
Mawein, Kook, 95

N

N'djili Airport, 83, 89
Nanking, 45
Ndibe, Okey, 1, iii, vii, 9, 27, 167, 186, 187
Ndlovu, Thabisani, 57, 68, 187
Niger Delta, 49, 50, 51, 52, 53, 54, 55, 56, 168
Nobel Prize, 49
North Kivu province, 18

O

Obasanjo, Olusegun, 51, 52, 56
Obi, Cyril I., vii, 10
Ogoniland, 53, 55
Onitsha, 29, 30, 185
Operation Mavhoterapapi, 108
Orientalism, 137, 153, 154, 156

R

Rhodesia Broadcasting Corporation, 34
Rwanda, 17, 18, 19, 23, 31, 50, 85, 105, 143, 153, 154, 155, 159, 171, 172, 173, 174, 175, 176, 177, 180, 181, 182, 186
Rwandan Patriotic Front, 179

S

Samuel, Karin, 171, 173, 175, 177, 178, 181, 182
Sese Seko, Mobutu, 84
Sierra Leone, 50, 159
Solzhenitsyn, A., 103
South Africa, 23, 81, 88, 96, 101, 104, 105, 123, 124, 129, 132, 133, 134, 173, 176, 181, 184, 186, 187, 188
Soyinka, Wole, 12, 27, 34, 42, 49
Sweden, vii, 9, 134, 184

T

Tanzania, 88, 158, 177
Toyota, 82, 86, 88

U

U.N. Food and Agricultural Organisation, 97
University of Zimbabwe, 60, 187
Uppsala, vii, 9, 10, 11, 12, 13, 131, 133

W

wa Thiongo, Ngugi, 47
War on Terror, 19, 137, 186
Woodman. Michael, 69, 188

Z

Zaïre, 81, 84, 87
Zebra Press, 171, 181, 182, 183
Zimbabwe African National Liberation Army, 57

www.ingramcontent.com/pod-product-compliance
Lightning Source LLC
Chambersburg PA
CBHW050804160426
43192CB00010B/1630